COASTAL STYLE

COASTAL STYLE

home decorating ideas inspired by seaside living

SALLY HAYDEN & ALICE WHATELY
photography by PAUL MASSEY

RYLAND
PETERS
& SMALL
LONDON. NEW YORK

DESIGNER Pamela Daniels

SENIOR EDITOR Henrietta Heald

LOCATION RESEARCH Emily Westlake

PRODUCTION Paul Harding
& Patricia Harrington

ART DIRECTOR Leslie Harrington

PUBLISHING DIRECTOR Alison Starling

STYLING Sally Hayden

TEXT Alice Whately

First published in 2008
This edition published in 2012
by Ryland Peters & Small
20–21 Jockey's Fields
London WC1R 4BW
and
519 Broadway
5th Floor
New York, NY 10012
www.rylandpeters.com

10 9 8 7 6 5 4 3 2 1

ISBN: 978-1-84597-616-3

A CIP record for this book is available from
the British Library.

Library of Congress Cataloging-in-
Publication Data
Hayden, Sally.
  Coastal style : home decorating ideas
inspired by seaside living / Sally Hayden
and Alice Whately ; photography by Paul
Massey.
    p. cm.
  Includes index.
  ISBN 978-1-84597-616-3
1. Interior decoration. 2. Seaside
architecture. I. Whately, Alice. II. Massey,
Paul. III. Title.
  NK2195.S43H39 2008
  747--dc22
                            2007047171

PRINTED IN CHINA

CONTENTS

INTRODUCTION

ALTHOUGH MOST PEOPLE ENJOY SPENDING TIME BY THE SEA – WALKING, SWIMMING OR SIMPLY RELAXING ON THE BEACH – SOME OF US EXPERIENCE THE PULL OF THE OCEAN TO SUCH A DEGREE THAT WE END UP ACQUIRING A COASTAL HOME. CERTAINLY, LIVING BESIDE THE SEA IS AN ENORMOUSLY ATTRACTIVE CONCEPT. THE NATURAL BEAUTY OF BIG SKIES AND VAST EXPANSES OF WATER PROVIDES A BLISSFUL ALTERNATIVE TO THE STRESSES OF 21ST-CENTURY LIFE, WHILE THE LAID-BACK COASTAL LIFESTYLE IS EQUALLY APPEALING. IT IS HARDLY SURPRISING, THEREFORE, THAT INCREASING NUMBERS OF US ARE MIGRATING TOWARDS THE OCEAN.

ESCAPE TO THE SEASIDE

The increasing popularity of coastal living has resulted in a growing interest in elegant, low-key interiors that reflect the relaxed simplicity of shoreside dwellings. Indeed, coastal chic is now taking a richly deserved turn in the spotlight, and the beautiful homes featured in this book – in locations ranging from New England to the Caribbean to Scandinavia – clearly demonstrate that the typically tasteful design of coastal interiors is as alluring as it is universal.

Coastal style has evolved from the myriad different ways in which seaside-dwellers have integrated the surrounding environment into their interiors. If you want to achieve this in your own home, big windows and sliding doors are highly desirable – as is a minimalist design scheme, which makes it possible for you to appreciate fully the views of sea, sand and sky. Paring back the furniture in your home also provides a calming reminder of the wide-open spaces beyond your window, while stripped wooden floors, streamlined storage and a unified colour scheme create a soothing, well-ordered impression.

A PALE, WATERY PALETTE AND MINIMALIST FURNISHINGS IN NATURAL MATERIALS SUCH AS WOOD AND STONE WILL REINFORCE THE SIMPLE APPEAL OF COASTAL ARCHITECTURE, REGARDLESS OF WHETHER YOU LIVE IN A SEASIDE COTTAGE OR A COLONIAL-STYLE VILLA.

Natural materials that reflect the seashore come into their own in coastal interiors. Driftwood furniture and tongue-and-groove wall cladding create a breezy, barefoot feel, while scrubbed flagstones recall the smooth sheen of surf-polished pebbles. To enhance the look, opt for a coastal palette: aqua blues, sea greens and oyster greys are ideal for achieving a watery look, while neutrals in shades of sand and shell recall the hues of the seashore. The occasional bolt of brilliant colour also works well in seaside interiors – scarlet, yellow and turquoise are all effective.

Establishing a sense of relaxed informality is one of the joys of coastal living. Although the seaside look is cool and classy, there is nothing precious about its decorative style. Instead, elegant eclecticism rules – with huge sofas, paint-flaked armoires, scrubbed tables and the odd chandelier set alongside faded kelims, rustic log baskets and nautical paintings propped up against the wall.

Decorative accessories, which take their cue from various coastal influences, are similarly spontaneous. Indeed, anything goes on the display front – from a massive model yacht in front of the fireplace to a display of straw hats randomly arranged on a wall. Fishing tackle, fossils and feathers are also popular, while the natural beauty of shells is unrivalled in terms of decorative embellishment.

Creating a comfortable and stylish outdoor space is one of the essential ingredients of coastal living. After all, if you live by the sea, you are going to want to spend lots of time enjoying natural environment. Again, the look is relaxed and laid-back – with furnishings ranging from streamlined loungers to solid, sunbleached tables and elegant parasols.

Coastal style is not only for people who live by the sea. Whatever type of home you have, from a high-rise apartment to a cottage in the country, you can establish a beachy feel. Simply follow this book's room-by-room guide to seaside chic, and you will discover the secrets of creating tranquil living areas, balmy bedrooms and shipshape kitchens.

THE ELEMENTS

ARCHITECTURE & DESIGN

THROUGHOUT HUMAN HISTORY, WATER HAS PROVED AN EXCELLENT COMPLEMENT TO BUILDINGS, INTENSIFYING THEIR SIGNIFICANCE AND STIMULATING ARCHITECTS AND DESIGNERS TO SCALE NEW IMAGINATIVE HEIGHTS. THE SEA, IN PARTICULAR, HAS LONG INSPIRED THE CONSTRUCTION OF INNOVATIVE BUILDINGS WHOSE PRINCIPAL DESIGN DIRECTIVE HAS BEEN TO MAXIMIZE THE JOYS OF LIVING ON THE COAST. LIKEWISE, THE MAIN PRIORITY OF DESIGNERS OF SEASIDE INTERIORS IS TO CREATE PRACTICAL AND AIRY LIVING SPACES THAT PROVIDE AN APPARENTLY SEAMLESS CONNECTION WITH THE SURROUNDING ENVIRONMENT.

BEAUTIFUL BEACH HOUSES

OPPOSITE:

TOP, LEFT TO RIGHT **The modernist design of a Long Island beach house by Stelle Architects capitalizes on stunning ocean views. Wraparound verandas are a dominant feature of colonial-style houses in the Caribbean. Locally quarried slate is a popular building material in Cornwall.**

MIDDLE, LEFT TO RIGHT **Outside walls painted in colours that reflect the sea and sky are a common sight in coastal homes. The wooden deck matches the building's walls, creating a sense of continuity. Houses with plenty of doors and windows to admit balmy breezes are vital in hot places.**

BOTTOM, LEFT TO RIGHT **The timber of wooden houses weathers to a soft silver through the action of salt, wind and sun. Some houses are painted bright white to deflect sunlight. A continuous strip of windows admits maximum light to a single-storey home, also designed by Stelle Architects.**

Although there are many different styles of architecture for people who live by the sea to choose from, one of the most coveted is the sprawling linear variety in which wood, glass and steel are used to enhance the effects of the shimmering light, salty air and changing weather conditions of coastal climates.

Concrete modernist houses, featuring large expanses of glass, represent another popular style, but, to avoid the brutalist look of raw concrete, many are painted white to impart a sense of visual freshness, as well as helping to deflect heat from the sun.

Seaside dwellings are most successful when the details of their architecture and construction have been planned in response to the local environment. For example, grand dwellings in the Caribbean – many of which imitate 18th-century neoclassical architecture of the colonial period – are characterized by louvred shutters, overhanging eaves and dormer windows, all of which reflect the need to promote air flow and give relief from the islands' hot and humid weather conditions.

Less expensive houses in the Caribbean – known by the locals as *cases* – feature clapboard cladding and steeply pitched roofs to protect the occupants from the scorching sun and heavy rain. Usually made from corrugated iron – one of the most common materials on the islands today – the roofs of *cases* are lightly nailed to the main frame of the house, so that, if a hurricane hits, they will come off easily and prevent the whole house from being blown away.

BELOW **The simple chic of a coastal home on Long Island is exemplified by smartly painted door and window frames, a couple of low-key deckchairs and a small wooden table.**

BELOW RIGHT **Steeply pitched roofs are an effective way to protect houses from sun and rain, as well as creating a homely feel that complements well-tended gardens full of trees and shrubs.**

BELOW FAR RIGHT **Clapboard exteriors are particularly popular in the north-eastern USA, where there is a plentiful supply of timber.**

In Scandinavia, where there is a long tradition of building recreational 'summer houses', beach architecture takes its cue from the generations of fishermen who built their homes of timber from the nearby pine and spruce forests. In response to the harsh winters, most timber-framed houses in Scandinavia, inland as well as on the coast, are sheathed in horizontal or vertical clapboarding (also known as weatherboarding) to protect the walls from the wind and rain, as well as adding extra insulation.

Clapboard houses also form an important part of the architecture of the New World, thanks to the European settlers who introduced traditional methods of timber-frame construction to North America's eastern seaboard at the beginning of the 17th century. To this day, the abundant supply of timber in Scandinavia and the USA has ensured that houses built from wood are still favoured over those built from brick and concrete.

Seaside homes elsewhere are also built using local resources. A cottage by the sea on the Norfolk

coast, for instance, is likely to be rendered in local brick and flint, while Mediterranean beach houses are often hewn from local stone such as limestone and granite, and feature marble floors, shuttered windows and small doors to ensure that interiors are kept dark, cool and shady.

Beach huts are also perennially popular. Springing up in Britain and elsewhere in the early 20th century, the original huts were intended as a changing facility for prim Edwardians of both sexes. Since then, these huts have become a much-loved feature of seaside towns all over the world. Indeed, their iconic status is such that prices have risen dramatically over the past decade – with many jewel-bright shacks now costing the same as a small house to buy.

Painted beach houses are far from new, however. Over the centuries, a variety of washes and paints have been used to colour, protect and decorate the exteriors of seaside homes. But while the palette favoured by those living in the chilly climes of Scandinavia is predominantly light and pallid,

BELOW LEFT TO RIGHT The beauty of sun-warmed blond wood can be appreciated in all its glory in this Danish seaside home, whose veranda underlines the building's rustic character. Slatted chairs and benches reinforce the linear look. The door shown below centre, which leads into an open-plan interior, is masterfully positioned to allow a glimpse of the sea through a large window at the opposite end of the house.

ABOVE **Antique wooden shutters opening onto a rough stone wall give a sense of nostalgic charm.**

ABOVE LEFT **A combination of cream walls, sea-green shutters and a peeling white picket fence offsets the severity of a grey slate roof.**

ABOVE FAR LEFT **Inlaid pebbles interspersed with pale brickwork give this cottage a genuinely quirky feel.**

BELOW AND OPPOSITE **Vertical and horizontal wooden boards are combined to harmonious effect in this English coastal home, which was built from two old railway carriages.**

houses in the Mediterranean sport vividly painted exteriors in rich blues and dense oranges. Equally colourful are the candy-hued *cases* that can be seen all over the islands of the Caribbean.

Different architectural styles apart, most coastal homes have been built to take as much advantage as possible of the maritime setting. Thus, sliding doors, skylights, picture windows and French windows predominate, as do balconies, verandas, decks and terraces.

Open-plan living areas are another important aspect of coastal design, evoking a sense of laid-back fluidity that reflects the informality of seaside living. That said, you don't have to have acres of space to create a feeling of flow. Simple adjustments such as replacing wood doors with glass-panelled ones, or ensuring that the flooring in your hall is the same as the flooring in your living area, are guaranteed to give even the smallest of coastal dwellings a sense of light and space.

FLOORS, WALLS & CEILINGS

RESILIENT, HARDWEARING FLOORS IN WOOD, STONE, SEAGRASS AND OTHER NATURAL MATERIALS ARE IDEAL FOR COASTAL INTERIORS. TIMBER REMAINS THE MOST POPULAR CHOICE FOR FLOORS, WALLS AND CEILINGS. SIMPLE WOODEN PLANKS, FITTED EITHER VERTICALLY OR HORIZONTALLY, OFFER AN UNRIVALLED SENSE OF FRESHNESS, WHILE PAINTED PANELS AND ARCHING RAFTERS GIVE A SIMILARLY AIRY FEEL. ROUGH STONE WALLS ARE ALSO EFFECTIVE IN SEASIDE HOMES, PARTICULARLY WHEN THEY FEATURE RANDOMLY SHAPED PIECES HEWN FROM LOCAL ROCKS.

BACK TO BASICS

OPPOSITE:

TOP, LEFT TO RIGHT **The patina of the untreated pillars contrasts well with the timber-clad walls and ceiling. A Neptune mosiac adds quirkiness to an outdoor passageway at the Hotel Tresanton in Cornwall. A distressed wooden frame complements the clean lines and flat colours of the portrait.**

MIDDLE, LEFT TO RIGHT **A slate floor, brick walls and a glass-panelled door make an intriguing textural mix. The smooth stone floor emphasizes the ruggedness of the brick walls. Painting walls and chairs in the same green gives cohesion to an all-wood interior.**

BOTTOM, LEFT TO RIGHT **The beachy tones of sandstone pavers give a sense of warmth, enhanced by a similar colour on the walls. Mosaic tiles recall old-fashioned swimming baths. An antique knotted rug adds interest to bleached floorboards.**

There is nothing like antique floorboards for adding character to a home, but they can be very expensive. If you plan to buy solid wood flooring and want a sense of Long Island airiness, go for pale woods such as ash, beech, maple or pine. For a Caribbean flavour, choose darker timbers such as fumed oak or iroko, while polished mahogany boards give an elegant Balinese feel.

If your budget is tight, restoring existing boards is the better option. Although messy and time-consuming, stripping and sanding creates an appropriately earthy look. You can disguise the imperfections of old boards with heavy-duty paint. Painting boards white is an easy way to make a space feel beachy-clean, while planks limewashed in powder blue or pale green recall streamlined Swedish interiors.

Stone floors – in the form of soft sandstone or Travertine flags – introduce a timeless solidity. Stone comes in many different colours, textures and patterns. Choose limestone for a laid-back Mediterranean feel or slate for a more rugged effect. The utilitarian appeal of polished concrete also works well in coastal interiors; tough and easy to clean, it can be painted white to create a modern Miami Beach feel.

Rugs add warmth to stone or wooden floors. Choose cotton dhurries in mellow colours to provide a soft focal point, or wool kelims to create textural contrast. Cheap rag rugs contribute a casual vibe to painted wooden floors, while hardwearing runners in dark colours are great for protecting high-traffic areas.

RIGHT Patterned tiles and the painted blue door and window frame enliven the entrance hall of the Hotel Tresanton. A straw hat sitting on an old church pew and a collection of oars and paddles create an antiquated feel.

OPPOSITE An unusual mix of brown and white gives cohesion to this restful eating area, also at the Hotel Tresanton. The texture of the wicker chairs is complemented by the smooth floor tiles, polished wood table and decorative yacht hulls on the wall.

Natural-fibre flooring offers a neutral base that is warm and textural. Sisal is tough but can be hard to clean, while coir and seagrass are similarly resilient but prickly underfoot. Softer materials, such as jute, work well in light-traffic areas. Other eco-friendly options include linoleum and cork. There are many colours and designs of linoleum to choose from, including photographic finishes depicting water and glistening pebbles. Cork is ideal for bathrooms, being impervious to water and soft to walk on.

Paint is the most popular finish in coastal homes. For a no-nonsense slick of colour, use water-based emulsion, the easiest and cheapest method of covering walls and ceilings. Tough, easy-to-clean eggshell and satin finishes are best used on surfaces vulnerable to marking, such as cupboard doors. Glossy finishes also make a smart contrast to opaque ones. For a chalky finish, use distemper or casein (milk) paint, while tinted colourwashes give a delightfully diluted hue. For a shimmery sparkle, pearlescent paints – which change colour depending on the angle and intensity of light – are perfect. You could also jazz up matt emulsion with a coat of opalescent paint for a sparkling, oceanic finish.

THE CALMING LINEARITY OF WOODEN
FLOORBOARDS HELPS TO ESTABLISH A
SENSE OF SPACE AND HARMONY.

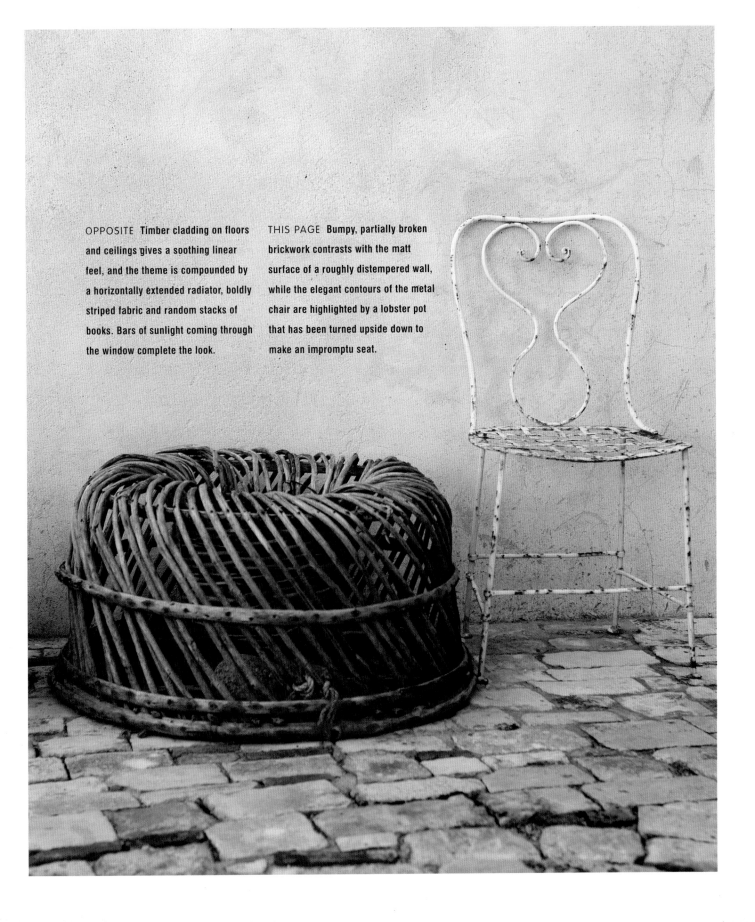

OPPOSITE **Timber cladding on floors and ceilings gives a soothing linear feel, and the theme is compounded by a horizontally extended radiator, boldly striped fabric and random stacks of books. Bars of sunlight coming through the window complete the look.**

THIS PAGE **Bumpy, partially broken brickwork contrasts with the matt surface of a roughly distempered wall, while the elegant contours of the metal chair are highlighted by a lobster pot that has been turned upside down to make an impromptu seat.**

NATURAL & ARTIFICIAL LIGHTING

ONE OF THE MAIN ATTRACTIONS OF LIVING BY THE SEA
IS THE LUMINOSITY OF THE LIGHT — A PHENOMENON
RARELY ENCOUNTERED INLAND. AS SEASIDE-DWELLERS
KNOW, THIS INTENSE RADIANCE IMPACTS ON EVERY
ASPECT OF COASTAL INTERIORS, FROM ARCHITECTURAL
DETAILS TO FURNITURE. ELECTRICAL LIGHT FITTINGS
IN THE COASTAL HOME ARE OFTEN A MIX-AND-MATCH
AFFAIR — WITH FLOOR AND TABLE LAMPS FAVOURED
OVER CONTEMPORARY UPLIGHTERS OR DOWNLIGHTERS.
MODERN CONTRIVANCES SUCH AS DIMMER SWITCHES
ARE FROWNED UPON, AS ARE UNDERFLOOR LIGHTING
AND, HEAVEN FORBID, FLUORESCENT STRIPS. INSTEAD,
ARTIFICIAL LIGHTING IS KEPT SIMPLE AND DIRECTIONAL.

LET THE SUN SHINE IN

OPPOSITE:

TOP, LEFT TO RIGHT **The starkly utilitarian appearance of a metal-mesh light adds interest to a stone wall. Glass chandeliers contrast elegantly with rustic furnishings and distressed paintwork. A lighthouse-shaped lamp reinforces the maritime mood.**

MIDDLE, LEFT TO RIGHT **Clear glass candle lamps, lit or unlit, make decorative display items. A simple vase is the ideal receptacle for a chunky candle anchored in a layer of variegated sand. Great accessories for seaside interiors, old-fashioned oil lamps cast an ambient glow.**

BOTTOM, LEFT TO RIGHT **A rusty storm lantern evokes an authentic seafaring feel, while the glass drops of an antique chandelier catch and reflect the light, helping to brighten up a dark hallway. Votive candles fit perfectly into small glass jars, and look best when hung in clusters of two or three.**

The direction in which a window faces has a radical effect on the type of natural light a room receives – an effect that is intensified in coastal homes. For example, an east-facing exposure gets strong light in the mornings, while those facing south-west receive direct light for most of the day. The shape and size of the windows are also important – with panoramic windows making it possible for the view to become part of the decor, and skylights harnessing light so that it pours in from above.

Doors and doorways – especially those giving access to gardens, decks and terraces – can also be used to usher light into an interior. These apertures, which are generally larger than other exits and entrances, offer a seamless connection between inside and out, particularly the sliding-door variety that feature large expanses of frameless glass. Alternatively, choose hinged French window styles, which fold back so that views are unimpeded.

The challenge in a coastal home is how to balance the practical aspects of a room with the way the natural light affects the decor. Your geographical location will also have a bearing on your design decisions. For example, the cool blue light of northern exposures gives colours and furnishings a defined look, while the golden light of southern and tropical localities dilutes neutral tones and softens harsh lines. The trick is to be aware of the quality and quantity of light in your home, and to decorate accordingly. If you live in a hot climate – or have a particularly sunny room – louvred blinds that can be adjusted to filter light as

required are ideal. Slatted shutters of the type found in the south of France or the Caribbean also work well, acting as an effective light barrier when closed and an excellent source of light and air when flung open. Simple Roman blinds, which can be hoisted to any height, are a subtle way to introduce colour, texture and pattern into an interior. You can add nautical allusions by choosing blinds made from hard-wearing sailcloth or neutral-coloured linens with a navy

BELOW, LEFT TO RIGHT **Traditional light fittings are much better suited to the slightly archaic style of coastal homes than contemporary designs. For best results, seek out lights with a simple seafaring feel such as these wall-mounted metal examples.**

OPPOSITE **Mixing different types of lighting can work very well, especially if the designs are at opposite ends of the style spectrum. At the Hôtel Le Sénéchal on France's Ile de Ré, a pair of substantial metal pendant lights flank a delicate chandelier, to create a look that is satisfyingly unique.**

trim – and underline the maritime theme by using cleats, eyelets and pulleys in place of traditional fixtures and fittings.

Unobtrusive roller blinds are perfect for maximizing the flow of air and light, since they can be raised to the very tops of windows, giving an unadorned, bare-faced feel. If you want to leave an exposure completely free from furnishings, you could always paint the window surrounds in a vibrant colour to inject definition and

LEFT AND FAR LEFT Louvred
shutters are among the most attractive
of window treatments. Their adjustable
slats make them satisfyingly functional,
allowing you to control the flow of
natural light, so that you get exactly
the required level of illumination.

OPPOSITE Leave floor-to-ceiling
windows free of curtains and blinds,
so that light can flood into your space.
Bare windows also provide the perfect
frame for watery vistas.

interest. For a romantic look, choose diaphanous drapes in floaty
materials such as voile or muslin. If you do opt for semi-transparent
drapes or scrims, however, remember that the sun's powerful rays
can cause serious damage to furniture and fabrics.

Simple and traditional are the watchwords when it comes to artificial
light in seaside homes. An Anglepoise lamp perched on top of a pile
of books on the floor is perfect, for instance, as are rustic table lamps
with shabby-chic shades or wall lights with an industrial edge.

Pendant lights are popular – their simple elegance reflecting the
clean lines of coastal living spaces. Choose antique chandeliers to
complement translucent colour schemes, or simple paper globes to
convey low-key simplicity. Pendant lights are also versatile, creating
an intimate feel when suspended low over a kitchen table, for example,
or serving as an arresting focal point when used as the central light
source in living rooms and bedrooms.

COLOUR

PART OF THE ALLURE OF LIVING BY THE SEA IS THE
WEALTH OF CALMING COLOURS THAT CHARACTERIZE
THE COASTAL LANDSCAPE. BY INCORPORATING AN
EQUALLY SOOTHING PALETTE IN OUR HOMES, WE CAN
CAPTURE A SIMILAR SENSE OF SERENITY. BETTER
STILL, THERE ARE NUMEROUS SOPHISTICATED SHADES
TO CHOOSE FROM — ALL OF WHICH TAKE ON A DEEPER
INTENSITY THROUGH THE ACTION OF OCEAN LIGHT.
BRINGING THE OUTSIDE IN BY OPTING FOR COLOURS
THAT REFLECT THE NATURAL ENVIRONMENT ENABLES A
SEAMLESS CONTINUITY OF THE BEACHY THEME.

WHITE ON WHITE

OPPOSITE:

TOP, LEFT TO RIGHT **A bowl of sandy-hued shells on a painted table makes a soothing still-life. A sky-blue door, flanked by earthenware pots, brightens the façade. The sea-green glaze emphasizes the aquatic feel of fish-shaped crockery.**

MIDDLE, LEFT TO RIGHT **A blue fridge, flanked by white units, is the focus of a simple kitchen; the colour theme is echoed in the striped pottery. Pebbles show various greys, from flint to palest marl. Silvery decking blends with the green of the window frames.**

BOTTOM, LEFT TO RIGHT **Blue and white is a popular pairing in coastal interiors, creating a sense of freshness and vitality that derives from the sea. Pots of young lavender and a vibrant green vine enhance the soft mauve of rustic shutters. The necklaces by Charlotte Lynggaard are reminiscent of sparkling coastal light.**

Creating an atmosphere of breezy informality is fundamental in coastal interiors, so plan to include large areas of white in any colour scheme. Many people shy away from the concept of living in a predominantly white space, fearing that it will either be cold and austere or, worse, bland and boring. In fact, the opposite is the case. There are literally hundreds of shades of white to choose from, many of which are inspired by the seashore. Pearlescent whites, for example, create a shimmering shell-like feel; bone whites are reminiscent of sunbleached flotsam and jetsam; while blue- and green-toned whites recall foam-flecked waves.

Whether you live in a seaside shack in the Caribbean or a modernist villa in Provence, introducing white into your home will make it seem lighter, airier and more invigorating. In order to prevent an all-white decorative scheme from seeming excessively sterile, it is advisable to combine shades of white that come from the same family, because the subtle mixing and matching of different tones will create layers of interest. The addition of different textures – a white wicker chair, a sleek contemporary table or a pale pleated lampshade, for example – will also help to diversify the look.

The advantages of living in an all-white interior are numerous. Not only do walls painted in pale shades make your space seem bigger and brighter, but continuity of colour also prevents fragmentation. If you live in a hot country, you can use silvery white to add a fresh oceanic feel, while creamier tones are an effective way to warm up beach houses in

ABOVE A cloudless blue sky lends brilliance to a classic-looking coastal home with white weatherboarding and shutters rendered in flaking turquoise emulsion. The effect is boldly cheerful, while the clash of colours recalls the hotel fronts of Miami Beach.

cooler regions. White interiors are also perfect for displaying artwork and ornaments, providing a blank canvas for showcasing maritime objects such as splashy modern seascapes, a collection of pale ceramics and delicate decorative items retrieved from the seashore.

As in the case of white, there is a vast spectrum of blues and greens for coastal homeowners to choose from. Washed-out shades of sea green, muted indigo and

cerulean blue are particularly effective in seaside interiors because they recall the watery world beyond your door. Limpid colours also harmonize with the shabby-chic style favoured by oceanside-dwellers, which features distressed paintwork and beaten-up old furniture.

Grey is another colour that works well in seaside interiors because it carries hints of misty horizons and endless pewter-

coloured seas. Formerly viewed as a rather uninspired choice for interior design schemes, grey is now being hailed as the colour *du jour*. And not before time. Offering a subtle spectrum ranging from pebble and oyster tones to light-reflecting steels, pearly silvers and sombre slates, grey imbues coastal interiors with the clean-washed sense of the seashore, as well as ushering in an air of cool sophistication. But bear in mind that natural light can have a dramatic effect on greys, so choose your shade carefully.

A naturally versatile colour, grey provides a calm, soothing complement to pale aquas, sea greens, rustic browns and, of course, white. Soft greys also help to offset the impact of stronger colours such as navy, yellow and terracotta, while weightier shades such as flint and slate are a great way to anchor interior design

ABOVE **Displaying maritime paintings is a straightforward way to introduce an impression of the seaside into your home. Combine them with other items, such as vases in delicate jade green, to complete an aquatic colour scheme.**

BELOW LEFT **A scarlet-upholstered sofa injects a brilliant bolt of colour into an otherwise beachy-toned living area, while the addition of a cotton throw on the sofa seat and the plain lines of the furniture prevent the red from becoming overwhelming.**

BELOW CENTRE **Red, white and black is an unusual colour scheme for a coastal interior, but this collection of objects, including a laquered pebble, a starfish and some vibrant-coloured coral, is reassuringly oceanic. The model car adds to the masculine feel.**

BELOW RIGHT **A white-framed mirror with seaweed details carved down both sides fits perfectly into the red-painted wall space behind it, while the sandy yellow of the exotic-looking birdcage does an effective job of softening the stark colour scheme.**

OPPOSITE **An open-fronted cabinet with 24 compartments makes an ideal showcase for a colourful mixture of shells in shades ranging from delicate silver to orange, green, purple and white. The dark wood helps to highlight the luminosity of the display pieces.**

schemes. If you are seeking a lighter look, choose luminescent silver greys that suggest shoals of tiny fish darting beneath the waves.

One advantage of creating a washed-out colour scheme is that it gives you the opportunity to include the occasional bold splash of colour and pattern. Hot summer blues such as azure and ultramarine are reminiscent of glamorous beach resorts, while nautical stripes in blue and white bring out the freshness and life-enhancing vitality of

OPPOSITE **The brilliant blue of the sea – which ranges from deep cerulean to transparent turquoise – is one of the main reasons that people are drawn to the Bahamas, a chain of low-lying islands, where pink and white sandy beaches dotted with palm trees predominate. The Bahamian skies are equally awe-inspiring, with frequent tropical storms resulting in dramatic cloud formations.**

the sea. Pattern and colour are most effectively incorporated into a scheme through the medium of soft furnishings. For example, in a plainly decorated room, a striped blind introduces an unexpectedly jaunty note, while a scattering of cushions in beach-towel brights or a rug in vivid hues will both make a striking focal point.

Soft, sandy colours also breathe life into coastal interiors. Like sea and sky colours, beachy tones look wonderful with almost any variety of white, while at the same time providing a visual link with the sunbleached landscape.

Grainy beiges are an excellent way to add warmth and texture to coastal homes; they are especially effective in larger dwellings, which may be in need of cosying up.

You can combine dune-coloured shades in oatmeal, biscuit and sand with dusty pinks to create an intimate, shell-like impression. More vibrant beach tones such as ochre, terracotta and coral are best reserved for feature walls, hallways and outdoor spaces, where they will provide a striking contrast to diluted shades of blue, green and grey.

Varieties of brown also play an important part in coastal colour schemes. Glossy mahogany, which calls to mind the deluxe interior of an expensive yacht, is a surefire way to add gravitas and weight to your interior spaces, while paler shades should be combined with silvery greys to evoke the soft, timeworn beauty of salt-stained wood.

TEXTURES & MATERIALS

TEXTURE IS AS SIGNIFICANT AS COLOUR AND PATTERN IN THE CREATION OF SUCCESSFUL DESIGN SCHEMES, ESPECIALLY COASTAL ONES, WHICH TEND TO BE COOLLY MINIMALIST. INDEED, THE RESTFUL SIMPLICITY OF SEASIDE HOMES — WITH THEIR LOW-KEY PALETTE AND ELEGANT FURNISHINGS — OFFERS THE PERFECT BLANK CANVAS FOR THE ADDITION OF TEXTURAL MATERIALS INSPIRED BY SEASHORE TREASURES. BUT BE WARNED: INTRODUCING TEXTURAL ELEMENTS CAN BE AS CHALLENGING A TASK AS CHOOSING WALLPAPER AND PAINT, ALTHOUGH THE RESULT — A HOME THAT IS AS TACTILE AS IT IS UNIQUE — IS WELL WORTH IT.

NATURAL SELECTION

OPPOSITE:

TOP, LEFT TO RIGHT **The fluid appearance of coral belies its abrasive texture. Tower shells threaded onto string draw attention to the elegant grain of a wooden chair. A clear-glass container perfectly complements the spiny skeleton of a starfish.**

MIDDLE, LEFT TO RIGHT **A random group of shells shows the spontaneous beauty of natural displays. The spiral ribs of an ammonite are enhanced by timeworn imperfections. Coral-, ivory- and grey-coloured shells in a stone bowl create a luminous effect.**

BOTTOM, LEFT TO RIGHT **A pair of shell necklaces, looped over a wooden pole, makes an intriguing juxtaposition between rough and smooth. The fine striations on a surf-battered conch shell offer an elegant contrast to the grainy sand, while a mass of tiny white shells, encased in large glass vases, give off a pearly illumination.**

The typical seaside interior includes myriad references to the textures, materials and colours of the maritime environment. These elements can be interpreted in many different ways. For example, if you want to create a sense of harmony, introduce similar textures such as gloss paint, sheer curtains and polished wood floors. Or, for a beachy feel, choose smooth stone flags reminiscent of surf-buffed pebbles, and combine them with swathes of soft fabric to recreate the silken beauty of the sea.

A tonal room with plain furnishings and a neutral palette provides the perfect backdrop for a variety of textural additions. Add a rattan sofa, unevenly painted dresser or patchwork quilt to create a lively feel, or furnish with tufty materials – a looped rug or a mohair throw – to give a sense of cosy rusticity. Texture can also be incorporated in more subtle ways: a semi-transparent panel hanging at a window will create light-filtered patterns on the floor, for instance, while a thoughtfully placed mirror will bounce images of different surfaces around the room.

Exploiting materials inherent in a building's architecture is another way to add textural depth. Stone, plaster or brick can be used to set the tone for a design scheme, while flooring – be it parquet, concrete or carpet – also has a major textural impact.

Creating a contrast between textures is challenging because there is such a wide choice of possible combinations. Layering different textures is one option, while contrasting two opposing textures, warm and cool, say, is both visually engaging and easy to achieve. You could, for

LEFT Wooden stanchions embedded in a rough concrete base have been transformed into an unusual piece of artwork, while a length of coiled rope that neatly binds them together completes the textural effect.

FAR LEFT The part-rough, part-smooth look of old driftwood replicates the myriad colours and grainy textures of the rippling waves of sand around it.

ABOVE Driftwood featuring a range of textures, grains and finishes makes a nice complement to the cracked and peeling paint of a simple wooden tray.

ABOVE LEFT Frondy flowers in a series of streamlined test-tube vases soften the cracked and salt-stained appearance of a piece of driftwood to make an eye-catching display in the home of the florist Jane Packer.

OPPOSITE Scant decoration is needed in rooms where wall and floor textures are the main focal point. Here, the rough stone cladding of the walls contrasts with the smooth surround of the fireplace and the slate floor tiles.

RIGHT Pebbles with holes in them can be used in decorative displays. Simply thread stones of a similar colour and size onto string and hang them up together with an occasional shell or piece of driftwood for contrast.

FAR RIGHT A simple line of pebbles makes an attractive windowsill display. Softly rounded pebbles look especially good on smooth surfaces, such as newly painted wood, while one or two rougher specimens add textural variety.

OVERLEAF, LEFT Two fabulous shell necklaces show the textural contrasts of the shore, one smooth and luminous, the other pitted and more detailed.

OVERLEAF, RIGHT Displaying a model boat carved from distressed wood on an equally timeworn timber shelf creates a unique coastal display.

example, decorate wooden shelves with a collection of glassware, or dress a wickerwork bed with a satin eiderdown. Combining rough and smooth textures is equally effective: metal wall-lights look great fixed onto bumpy stone walls, as does a lump of knobbly coral displayed beneath a sleek glass dome.

Furniture, especially wooden styles, also adds textural variety. The soft patina of wood bleached by the sun is perfect for coastal homes – its light, silvery appearance recalling the surf-smoothed environs of the seashore. Similarly, driftwood can imbue a home with a rugged feel, its knots, bumps and whorls creating a splendidly sculptural effect.

Waxed wooden furniture enhances feelings of warmth and rusticity, while the glassy patina of varnished wood gives a clean colonial feel. Sleek woods such as mahogany respond beautifully to polishing and work best in restful spaces such as bedrooms or studies. For best results, combine mahogany with other cool textures such as freshly

ABOVE **Similar materials can be paired as effectively as contrasting ones. Here, the silvery slats of a simple wooden chair provide the perfect complement to similarly salt-stained timber cladding.**

ABOVE RIGHT **One advantage of wooden decking is that it grows more attractive the longer it is exposed to the elements; here, smooth striations have been etched by wind and sun.**

starched linen, simple glass carafes and elegant silverware. The intricate weave of rattan, cane and wicker furnishings also suits coastal interiors and provides a pleasing contrast to smoother surfaces such as tongue-and-groove panelling or flat-weave upholstery.

Blistered paint surfaces evoke memories of old fishing boats, paint-flaked beach huts and derelict lighthouses. Peeling paint that reveals patches of wood underneath is particularly attractive, while flaking paint gives a venerable appearance to metal furnishings such as radiators or delicate wrought-iron planters.

Leather is another tactile material, which becomes softer with age. Leather furniture, in the form of squashy sofas and cosy club chairs, is ideal for creating a warm atmosphere, particularly in cooler climates where icy gales and damp sea mists prevail.

Wrought-iron and metal furniture combines elegance and durability. Sought-after pieces include curvy metal daybeds, pretty café-style tables and curlicued metal chairs. For best results, upholster daybeds in a chic French fabric – a toile de Jouy beach scene is ideal – or tie seat pads made from striped ticking to the backs of metal chairs.

ABOVE **A single coat of paint on a timber-clad house allows the grain to show through, creating a rough-and-ready look reminiscent of traditional clinker-built boats and ships.**

ABOVE LEFT **Overgrown bushes soften the textures of this crumbling façade, where pitted wood, cracked concrete and rusty corrugated iron create an inspirational combination of weathered building materials.**

FABRICS

WHILE COMFORT IS OFTEN A SUBTLE, UNDERSTATED
FEATURE OF COASTAL HOMES, THERE IS NO NEED TO
COMPROMISE ON THE CHOICE OF SOFT FURNISHINGS.
QUALITY RATHER THAN QUANTITY IS THE KEY, WITH
CHIC, SIMPLE MATERIALS TAKING PRECEDENCE OVER
SUMPTUOUS SWAGS OR FROU-FROU PILLOWS. FABRICS
WITH MARITIME MOTIFS SUIT THE RELAXED APPROACH
OF SEASIDE DECORATING SCHEMES, WHILE MIXING
AND MATCHING DESIGNS IS ALSO EFFECTIVE — BUT
REMEMBER THAT THE MATERIALS YOU SELECT MUST
BE HARD-WEARING AND WASHABLE, SO THAT THEY CAN
WITHSTAND THE RIGOURS OF COASTAL LIVING.

TACTILE TOUCHES

TOP, LEFT TO RIGHT **A silk-knit cushion in pale aqua reflects the light, suggesting luxury, while a rough wool blanket makes a good textural contrast to smooth wood. Cushions in cool linen echo the soft shades of sandy shores.**

MIDDLE, LEFT TO RIGHT **Feminine bedlinen with a pattern combining tiny florals and sky-blue stripes enlivens a beachside boudoir. A tassled hessian throw lends a look of casual elegance. Upholster cushions and thin mattresses in durable cotton ticking – and you'll have the perfect excuse to lounge around all day at home.**

BOTTOM, LEFT TO RIGHT **Striped fabrics add a smart, shipshape feel to coastal spaces. A cushion embroidered with a fish motif by Jan Constantine enhances the quirky appeal of a chair seat bound in rope. Antique linen becomes softer and more attractive with each passing year.**

To create a successful soft furnishings scheme in a seaside home, take your cues from the textures and colours of nature. Fabrics such as nubbly linens, rough hessian and watered silk are perfect for bringing the outdoors inside, while a palette of sky blues, cloudy whites and soft greys creates a soothing harmony in a coastal setting.

Although plain textural fabrics should be the foundation of your design scheme, introducing an occasional splash of pattern is a good way to prevent an interior from appearing too tonal. Fabric designs that incorporate blowsy florals or bold Regency stripes are not a good idea, however. Instead, go for simple tickings, ginghams or small-scale florals that reflect the informal character of seaside style.

Cotton is a favoured fabric in coastal interiors, because of its crisp appearance and lightness. Available in various textures and forms including cotton canvas, brushed cotton, towelling, calico and denim, cotton is wonderfully versatile and can be used for a wide range of decorative purposes, from bedding to curtains. When buying cotton fabrics, pay as much as you can afford, because the more expensive the material, the softer and more appealing it will become over time.

Linen is another fabric that ages well. Available in natural colours including ivory, tan, grey and green, linen is especially desirable in hot climates since it stays a degree or two below room temperature. Linen also resists dirt, and can hold up to 20 per cent of its own weight in moisture without feeling damp, making it ideal for humid conditions too.

ABOVE AND OPPOSITE **A felt cushion designed by Jan Constantine introduces a nautical edge, while contrasting fabrics look good together on a plain sofa. The sailors' uniforms pressed behind glass frames reinforce the maritime theme.**

ABOVE RIGHT **A bold red, white and blue colour scheme gives this bedroom a patriotic feel. The sense of cohesion is based on the mixing and matching of Jan's quirky cushions and blankets.**

Along with other coarse-textured fabrics such as hessian and jute, linen combines easily with different textiles and tends to work best in rustic-looking homes where wood, slate and stone also feature. If you like shabby-chic interiors, go for antique textiles, which will enhance the faded charm of distressed paintwork, second-hand furniture and mix-and-match colour schemes. There are many timeworn fabrics to choose from, including lace tablecloths, tartan rugs and embroidered wall hangings. Mix old-fashioned fabrics with a few accent pieces such as a hand-knitted cushion or a patchwork quilt to complete the eclectic look.

Like cotton, silk is a fabulously versatile fabric that can be used to equal effect in hot and cool climates. Silk's slippery-soft properties mean that it works well in bedrooms, where a high-level of comfort is required. Use it for curtains or bedlinen, where its elegant drape will introduce a languorous feel, or, for a romantic look, combine it with

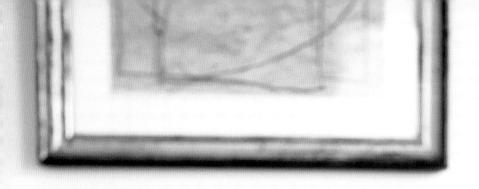

THIS PAGE **When choosing fabrics, look for versatile materials that will work as well inside as they do out. Here, a smart black and white striped mattress with a matching cushion provide a nice contrast to cool blue walls and an abstract print. However, the tough canvas fabric could be used to equal effect outdoors, softening the lines of a deckside lounger, for instance, or bringing a touch of elegance to a swinging hammock.**

gossamer-fine fabrics such as mosquito netting, muslin and voile. Watered silk, available in a range of washed-out coastal colours, looks similarly good in bedrooms, its tidemark pattern recalling waves lapping on the shore. Cosier fabrics such as sheepskin, wool, felt, velvet and suede are particularly effective in homes prone to cold and damp. The tactile appeal of densely woven fabrics is perfect for monotonal rooms, where the introduction of differently textured materials brings subtle

layers of interest. You can also create a sense of relaxed sophistication through the addition of rugs, cushions and throws. A cashmere blanket tossed over the back of a leather armchair gives an impression of traditional elegance, for example, while squashy knitted cushions will soften the rigorous lines of modern sofas. Plain floors, especially of the tiled, stone or concrete variety, also benefit from material relief. Warm up cool slate tiles with a sheepskin rug, for instance, or cheer up a dark passageway with a colourful cotton runner.

ABOVE, LEFT TO RIGHT **Jan Constantine's cushions featuring seaside motifs such as yachts and gulls strike a light-hearted note, while thick cotton curtains featuring a mixture of striped and checked fabrics are similarly cheerful, adding warmth and a sense of antiquity.**

DISPLAY & EMBELLISHMENT

THE OCEANS ARE A SOURCE OF COUNTLESS BEAUTIFUL ITEMS THAT CAN BE PUT TO DECORATIVE USE, BUT PEBBLES, SHELLS AND CORAL SHOULD BE ACQUIRED ONLY WITH PROPER REGARD FOR THE ENVIRONMENT. COLLECTIONS OF ANTIQUE SHELLS AND PIECES OF CORAL ARE ACCEPTABLE, OF COURSE, BUT A HOARD OF EXOTIC MARINE TREASURES IS NOT NEEDED TO CREATE AN ARRESTING DISPLAY. SIMPLE FINDS SUCH AS ROSY SUNSET SHELLS, TEXTURAL SCALLOPS AND SILVERY-GREEN LIMPETS CAN BE FREELY PICKED UP ON BEACHES AROUND THE WORLD — AND ARE JUST AS ATTRACTIVE AS THEIR MORE RAREFIED COUSINS.

THE
ISLAND
OF
THE COLORBLIND

BRIAN KEITH JACKSON THE VIEW FROM HERE

Henry Louis Gates, Jr.

JUBILEE

The Founding of Evil Hold School N.Tolstoy

Robert McCrum

W.H. Allen

INTRINSIC BEAUTY

Since pebbles and shells are so intrinsically beautiful, you can display them with a minimum of fuss. A line of smooth grey stones is a great way to embellish a plain windowsill, for example, while a cheap goldfish bowl filled with cowrie shells is similarly alluring. Shoreline treasures are also eye-catching when arranged on a table or tray, particularly if you leave enough space between the objects to create a sense of symmetry. Feathers, starfish and strands of dried seaweed can be used to add texture and form to display schemes, while items such as driftwood and fossils are easily fashioned into shelves, lamp bases and bookends.

Delicate glass shelves – or cabinets with glass doors – are one of the most effective ways of displaying marine finds. Not only does glass complement their fragility, but its light-reflecting qualities also enhance the luminosity of shells and coral, so that they glow in the sun.

Tidal treasures also make excellent embellishments for furniture and furnishings. Drawer handles in the form of whelks or cockles are a perennial favourite, while lampshades fringed with tiny pheasant shells add a touch of frivolity. For sparkle and shine, include mother-of-pearl boxes or photograph frames in your decorative arrangements or scour antiques markets for 19th-century mirrors with shell-encrusted frames.

Coastal homes also benefit from nautical references. Storm lanterns, barometers, telescopes, binoculars – even a pair of paint-flaked oars – will introduce a seafaring note, while sun-faded flags and old-fashioned maps or shipping charts offer a similarly effective maritime feel.

BELOW, LEFT TO RIGHT Angling equipment adds a flavour of the sea. Mixing and matching ornaments is a good display technique, but keep to a single theme. A portrait of a naval captain introduces a 'sea dog' feel, while the macho appeal of this display is underlined by the seemingly casual addition of a model motor boat.

Model yachts are much-favoured ornaments in coastal homes, helping to brighten up fireplaces, mantelpieces and bookshelves. Boats made out of driftwood also look attractive, while reclaimed signage or a souvenir ship in a bottle adds a kitsch element. If your home needs an injection of colour, a display case filled with medals on brightly striped ribbons will do the trick, while a discarded lifebelt or faded orange buoy are perfect for jazzing up exterior spaces.

OPPOSITE Similarly themed nautical paintings make a dramatic impact when displayed against a combination wall of roughly hewn stone and smooth wood panelling. An upright fishing rod acts as a balance to the horizontal lines of the pictures.

Not surprisingly, fish images and motifs are very popular among seaside-dwellers. Whether you want dolphins dancing across your duvet or swordfish on your splashback, there will be a company with the products to satisfy your needs. Brightly coloured floats, reels, flies, lures and other fishing tackle also look good in coastal homes, introducing a gritty, workmanlike feel that makes a nice contrast to softer details such as sun-bleached linens and delicate coral sprays.

Nautical artwork – from sepia ship prints to modern seascapes – is a must in coastal homes. Prop pictures on a mantelpiece or shelves and arrange shoreline finds around them. A faded yacht-print surrounded by surf-smoothed stones and textured ceramics in beachy shades is ideal for creating an impression of casual chic, while chunky box frames make an informal display case for starfish, shells and other marine objects.

When hanging pictures, remember that frames of different sizes look great grouped together as long as the content and the colouring are roughly the same. If you want to create a montage of seaside images, it's worth abiding by a few rules. For example, feature no more than three colours. Keep your montage free from the constraints of symmetry to achieve a mood of relaxed spontaneity. Overlap pictures to give an informal feel, and juxtapose close-up shots with some full-sized images. Although creating an attractive montage is not as easy as it looks, trial and error will almost certainly yield successful results.

ABOVE **A clutch of suitcases, piled one on top of another, is an unusual alternative to shelves or bookcases. For best results, choose designs that are similar in style and colour.**

ABOVE LEFT AND FAR LEFT **Glassware can be relied on to make a striking display, especially if the shapes are varied but the colours are the same. A haphazard selection of candlesticks in light-reflective metals introduces a touch of glamour.**

OPPOSITE **To make their visitors feel relaxed and at home, David Flint Wood and India Hicks have installed a three-dimensional mixed-media 'scrap wall'. in the writing area of their guest house.**

ABOVE Bookshelves don't have to be neat in order to look attractive. Here, two solid chunks of driftwood add interest to a haphazardly filled shelf featuring battered-looking paperbacks.

ABOVE LEFT On a shelf above an archway, David Flint Wood and India Hicks have set up a 'lending library of hats'. It consists of hats donated by past guests for use by future guests.

LEFT Hanging a selection of hats on the wall will give your interior a quirky feel, as well as offering an excellent alternative to paintings or mirrors. For best results, choose hats that are soft and obviously well worn.

FAR LEFT Fishing tackle makes an arresting display, thanks to the variety of shapes, materials and occasional splashes of brilliant colour.

THIS PAGE **For maximum effect, display natural objects on distressed rather than shiny surfaces. Here, shells and a candle in a metal bowl complement a rough wooden table.**

OPPOSITE **A pretty paint-flaked chair provides the perfect setting for a subtle display in which a few delicate blooms in a clear-glass vase create an essential focal point.**

STONES, SHELLS AND OTHER NATURAL FINDS LOOK ALLURING ARRANGED ON A TABLE OR SIMPLE RATTAN TRAY.

RIGHT The washed-out colours of an antique cupboard set the tone for this simple display, which includes an eclectic mix of postcards that echo the white, blue and grey colour scheme. Pebbles and shells in similar hues make a nice finishing touch.

FAR RIGHT Randomly arranged bunches of flowers bring distressed furnishings such as a mottled mirror or a paint-chipped metal table to life. A simple bowl of tiny shells completes the rustic scene.

OPPOSITE An unframed portrait of a young man in a nautical top gives this otherwise pristine interior a slightly edgy feel, while the horizontal slats of the blinds echo the sitter's striped T-shirt and the stark lines of the chair.

Raffia baskets, sun hats, children's buckets and spades and other beach essentials can also be used decoratively in coastal interiors. A wooden tub filled with parasols, shrimping nets and beach balls will enliven a hallway, for example, while a surfboard with brightly coloured detailing or a wooden peg rail for towels cheers up an outdoor space. You could hang bunting across doorways or make a decorative feature of straw hats by hanging them all together on randomly placed hooks.

Fresh flowers breathe light and life into an interior. Without them, however accomplished your design scheme, the space will feel dead and uninhabited. Rambling roses, camellias, gardenias, hydrangeas and similar old-fashioned blooms harmonize with northerly coastal interiors, while spiky cacti or vivid bougainvillea suit homes in hotter climates. In coastal homes, simple ceramic jugs or clear glass vases make the best receptacles for flowers, while galvanized pails and single-stem containers also enhance the casual feel.

THE SPACES

LIVING SPACES

THE COASTAL LIVING ROOM IS A SPLENDIDLY INFORMAL AFFAIR, FEATURING AN ECLECTIC MIX OF FURNISHING STYLES, FOUND OBJECTS AND DRAMATIC ARTWORKS. AS IN OTHER ROOMS, THE FEELING OF SPONTANEITY IS THE RESULT OF CAREFUL EDITING, IN WHICH ELEMENTS OF THE NATURAL WORLD ARE PERMITTED TO TAKE CENTRE STAGE. IN THIS WAY, STRIPPED WOODEN FLOORS, BARE WALLS, OPEN LOG FIRES AND A SIMPLE BEACHY PALETTE PREDOMINATE, WHILE FABRICS ARE KEPT TO A MINIMUM AND LIGHTING COMES FROM A MIXTURE OF LARGE, DRAMATIC WINDOWS AND A FEW STRATEGICALLY PLACED FLOOR AND TABLE LAMPS.

BRINGING THE OUTSIDE IN

Designing your living room in such a way that the sea and sky become an integral part of the décor should be straightforward, since most coastal houses have many exposures, including sliding doors, picture windows and skylights – all of which help to forge a link between inside and out. A large picture window is the most enviable of these, making

a delightful focal point around which to base design schemes. Arrange seating to take full advantage of both the light and the view, and keep the room free of clutter, so as not to detract from the drama outside.

Although coastal homes can take an eclectic range of furnishings, coordinated seating helps to anchor a large living room. Rooms with grand, evenly spaced windows also benefit from similarly styled seating, preferably arranged in rectangular or boxy shapes to echo the

RIGHT **A wood-burning stove is a strong focal point in a cream-coloured living space, which was fashioned from an old railway carriage on the Sussex coast. The look is enlivened by a collection of wooden seabirds and a scattering of Lloyd Loom armchairs.**

OPPOSITE **Combining square and rectangular shapes with softer, more rounded ones creates a soothing symmetrical look, while the use of a restrained colour scheme featuring shades of white, brown, black and grey evokes a modern minimalist feel.**

size and regularity of the windows. If you have a large, square expanse of glass, put a long, low-slung sofa directly beneath it as a linear counterpoint. If your living space has few or small windows, you can be bolder in your choice of seating. For example, a chaise longue in front of French windows creates a languorous feel, while a cosy basket chair near a window with plenty of direct light invites you to curl up with a good book.

Window treatments should be strictly pared down. Opt for simple curtains or semi-transparent blinds in plain cotton or linen weaves, or choose streamlined louvred slats that enable you to control the flow of light. If you have stunning views, and are fortunate enough not to be overlooked, leave windows bare.

Lack of adornment is another feature of coastal living spaces, with simple floor and wall treatments leading the way. Bare or painted floorboards have a calming linearity that is unrivalled in creating a sense of harmony; they can also withstand heavy traffic.

Scour antique shops and flea markets for pieces of furniture that combine informality and elegance.

AN OPEN FIRE OR SIMPLE WOOD-
BURNING STOVE REINFORCES THE
ELEMENTAL QUALITY THAT LIES AT
THE HEART OF COASTAL STYLE.

ABOVE **Plain sofas, a simple coffee table and an antique kelim are all the decoration needed in a large living space, where the view through French windows provides most of the interest.**

RIGHT, TOP TO BOTTOM **A glass-panelled door and white-painted floorboards help to create a feeling of airiness and light, while pale fabrics and a few carefully selected pieces of** furniture enhance the look. Curvilinear wicker chairs, complete with blue and white striped cushions, give a beachy feel, as does a cluster of fishing rods casually propped up in the corner. An

office area, relegated to the corner of
a large living room, showcases coastal
chic in the form of a sandy-coloured
butterfly chair, a pale streamlined desk
and a selection of orchids.

OPPOSITE In their spectacular sitting room in the Bahamas, David Flint Wood and India Hicks have created a unified theme by arranging an enormous fan of palm fronds beside an oil painting depicting coconut trees. Firewood is contained in wicker and sisal storage baskets.

ABOVE Displaying pebbles and shells is not the only way to evoke a maritime mood. Here, polished oars, a pair of binoculars and a black and white yachting print do the job just as well.

ABOVE RIGHT Simple ornaments such as an ammonite and an elegant wooden model of a seabird create an aura of calm in this work space, while the flat expanse of water outside the window enhances the meditative feel.

OVERLEAF A large, well-proportioned living room designed by Tom Scheerer is the setting for statement furniture such as a vast white coffee table and outsized sofas. Red coral branches are among the striking decorative items.

Comfortable seating is the most important aspect of seaside living spaces. Pair classic sofas with sprawling armchairs, or opt for a single super-size sofa with a crumpled cotton cover to convey a luxurious lived-in impression. Wicker chairs provide a textural complement to smartly upholstered sofas, while easy-to-wash loose covers and scatter-back sofas, distinctive for their large number of randomly arranged cushions, both suggest informality and spontaneity.

Fabrics in coastal living spaces are casual and utilitarian. Canvas, cotton, linen, twill and denim all fit the bill, while softer textures such as cashmere or crushed velvet can be introduced in the form of throws or shawls tossed over the backs of sofas and chairs.

Seaside living is synonymous with simplicity – a fact that should be reflected in the materials and textures you choose for your living room. No matter the size of the space, natural elements should reign supreme, with tables and chairs reflecting the grainy qualities of the shoreline. Whitewashed wood, weathered basketweave and distressed metal

THIS PAGE **David Flint Wood and India Hicks** have combined antique and new pieces to great effect in the Long Room of their Pavilion for guests in the Bahamas. A 21st-century abstract drawing hangs behind an 18th-century gilded chair, and vintage white tennis balls are displayed in a modern idiom. The successful mixture of disparate items depends on tonal harmony.

OPPOSITE:

ABOVE AND BELOW LEFT **The** dramatic scale of this birdcage is emphasized by the dark wood chairs on either side. A mirror hung opposite a doorway brightens a dark space.

ABOVE AND BELOW CENTRE **Flint Wood and Hicks** have used light from a window to show why this piece by Philippe Starck is called a Ghost chair. Louvred shutters control light flow in living areas with many windows, while a heavy table anchors the scheme.

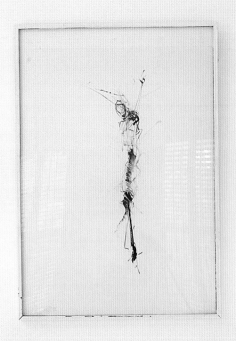

are all ideal, while age-spotted mirrors and glass-topped tables are great for maximizing light and space. Choose floor and table lamps in preference to modern spotlights or downlighters, since lamps will give an ambient glow that is in tune with the informal coastal mood.

An open fire or simple wood-burning stove completes the scene, as well as providing an indispensable source of heat in homes that are subject to the vagaries of cold sea mists.

TOP **An elegant lamp with a clear-glass stand is a subtle way of making this interior seem lighter and brighter.**

ABOVE **The cool, colonial feel of tongue-and-groove walls is enhanced by a central ceiling fan, a large potted palm, and black and white photographs artfully arranged on the wall.**

COOKING & EATING SPACES

KITCHENS AND DINING AREAS IN HOMES BESIDE THE SEA FEATURE A FEW CAREFULLY CHOSEN FIXTURES AND FITTINGS THAT REFLECT THE RUSTIC INFORMALITY TYPICAL OF COASTAL STYLE. ALTHOUGH THE LOOK IS CHARMINGLY REMINISCENT OF PAST TIMES, THERE IS NOTHING REMOTELY ARCHAIC ABOUT THE LAYOUT, WHICH CELEBRATES THE FASHION FOR AMALGAMATING COOKING AND EATING AREAS INTO A SINGLE OPEN-PLAN SPACE. MODERN COASTAL KITCHENS ARE ALSO LIKELY TO FEATURE A VARIETY OF HOMELY ADDITIONS SUCH AS OPEN LOG FIRES, COMFORTABLE ARMCHAIRS, THE OCCASIONAL SOFA AND A RANGE OF DECORATIVE ITEMS INCLUDING PICTURES, LAMPS AND MIRRORS.

EASY RUSTICITY

To create a lived-in feel in your coastal kitchen, incorporate a mixture of textures such as wood, galvanized metal, glass, linen and laminate, and pair old and new, such as tongue-and-groove panelling with moulded plastic chairs. Wood enhances warmth and cosiness, and, despite its porosity, is very clean, making it ideal for work surfaces, dining tables and chopping boards. For best results, choose temperate hardwoods such as oak, beech and maple, which are strong and easy to maintain.

Coastal cooking and eating areas should be calm and uncluttered, but fitted kitchens are not advised, since they may make the space look cold and clinical. Instead, choose a few freestanding pieces of furniture and keep paraphernalia such as blenders and microwaves out of sight.

If your cooking and eating area has little natural light, try to amplify the light that is available. This is best achieved by painting the walls a pale colour – white or off-white is ideal – to convey a functional air.

THIS PAGE **Natural materials such as distressed wood and rough stone bring a sense of homeliness to this Ile de Ré kitchen. The freestanding furniture adds to the lived-in look.**

OPPOSITE **The sturdy yet timeworn character of this fireplace and hearth have a rustic appeal, while a group of vintage pots and pans and a Shaker-style broom complete the scene.**

OVERLEAF **Position your table by a window so that you can enjoy the view while you eat. Sunlight and a cooling sea breeze will also heighten the pleasure of dining close to nature.**

Finishing cupboards, skirting boards and cabinets in a gloss paint will make your space seem brighter; you can achieve a similar effect with light-reflective flooring such as ceramic tiles, linoleum or pale scrubbed flagstones. It is also possible to harness light by introducing metal accents. For example, installing stainless-steel worktops and suspending shiny aluminium pans from a rail are subtle ways of intensifying natural illumination, while other reflective materials such as enamel, mirror, glass and Perspex will also help to bounce light around the room.

Conversely, cooking and eating areas in which light is abundant are best furnished with absorbent materials that have the effect of softening the glare.

OPPOSITE:

ABOVE LEFT Cream crockery spilling out of a glass-fronted cabinet adds interest to an all-white cooking space.

ABOVE CENTRE Sleek minimalist furnishings such as floorboards and an elegant breakfast bar complement stunning sea views.

ABOVE RIGHT Glamorous retro-style wallpaper and a lustrous table lamp liven up a streamlined kitchen.

OPPOSITE:

BELOW LEFT White paint and plain furnishings open up small spaces.

BELOW CENTRE A dark wood cabinet makes a perfect display case for a collection of glassware.

BELOW RIGHT White fixtures and fittings help to amplify light and space in a small kitchen that might otherwise appear dark and poky.

THIS PAGE An antique candelabra makes a dramatic complement to a set of Eiffel chairs by Charles Eames and a minimalist modern painting.

RIGHT AND FAR RIGHT **Cards and photographs hang from delicate wire prongs designed by the jeweller Charlotte Lynggaard. Shiny floorboards, cane chairs and a small chandelier add interest to a white dining area.**

OPPOSITE **Blond-wood furnishings and an open log fire give this high-ceilinged kitchen a light, airy feel. The central dining table is flanked by Hans Wegner's Wishbone chairs.**

Roughly plastered walls and slate floors, for example, are effective, along with seagrass matting, dark wood cabinets and cane or wicker chairs. Storing cutlery or mats in wicker baskets also reduces reflection, as does the addition of other light-absorbing elements such as densely woven fabrics or opaque glassware.

A variety of looks, from warm and homely to cool and linear, suit cooking and eating spaces in seaside homes. Retro kitchens with 1950s-style pieces and casual kitchen/diners that recall chic holiday homes are both among the most popular. If your space is large, you will probably want to divide it into zones for cooking, dining and living. This can be done by artful placement of one or two dramatic freestanding pieces; Welsh dressers, pastel-painted armoires or large cabinets with glass or wire mesh panels are all

ideal. Comfortable sofas and chairs with hardwearing loose covers in fabrics such as denim or cotton twill will enhance the multi-functional feel. You can also create distinct zones by using a variety of electric lighting systems, which will allow you to shift the focus of attention from cooking to relaxed dining at the flick of a switch. To achieve visual flow in open-plan spaces, install the same flooring throughout.

Regardless of the size of your space, the table you furnish it with is likely to become the central feature. Large, refectory-style tables with long benches suit large dining areas, while benches or banquettes are equally effective in smaller eating areas, where there may not be much room to push chairs in and out. The position of the table is also key. If you have enough space, put it in the centre

ABOVE, ABOVE LEFT AND ABOVE FAR LEFT The decorative theme at florist Jane Packer's home near the east coast of England is based on traditional rusticity, while a line of pebbles on a windowsill and a mirror in a driftwood frame recall the beach. Quirky details and old-fashioned crockery add character to the kitchen. A vintage draining board and chipped enamel jug give a retro impression.

LEFT Retro accessories such as antique canisters and standard-issue glass tumblers are guaranteed to give a kitchen a chic, utilitarian feel.

FAR LEFT Monotone kitchens are most successful when the windows frame a captivating view. Here, the foliage in a pretty walled garden complements the plain furnishings and green and white décor.

RIGHT **A nautical chart covered by a simple Perspex panel injects a subtle seafaring feel into a dining area, while votive candles displayed in clear glass vases are coolly elegant.**

OPPOSITE **Introducing a variety of textures into an all-white interior prevents the space from appearing bland and lifeless. In Tom Scheerer's scheme in the Bahamas, louvred cupboard doors and woven raffia chairs complement a shiny laminate table and glossy wall chart.**

of the room, where it will have maximum impact, or near a window or French window, so that you can enjoy the fresh air and sea views.

To create a cool linear kitchen, combine lashings of pale paint with tongue-and-groove panelling and well-disguised storage. A few eclectic furnishings will inject interest and character; directors' chairs give streamlined spaces a funky feel, while a chandelier adds a touch of glamour. Layering white on white is another useful technique, but include a textural element: replacing plain door panels with louvred styles or incorporating crumpled linen curtains or crenellated crockery will enliven a monotone space, for example. Retro furnishings such as reproduction 1950s-style cookers and curvy enamel fridges in pastel shades are particularly effective in smaller cooking and eating spaces. Alternatively, scour architectural salvage yards for reconditioned butlers' sinks, draining boards and taps, and use vintage fabric to curtain off storage areas. Accessories such as old-fashioned tea kettles, antique caddies and cream enamelware complete the look.

INSTEAD OF A FITTED KITCHEN
AND DINING AREA, OPT FOR A FEW
FREESTANDING PIECES TO CREATE
A RELAXED, ECLECTIC FEEL.

BELOW, LEFT TO RIGHT **A collection of crockery can make an appealing display, especially when piled up on an artfully distressed table. Old-fashioned hooks work well in rustic kitchens; paint them in a washed-out colour to add a coastal feel. Timeworn timber tables suit the informality of coastal dining spaces.**

Decorative items can be included in cooking and eating areas, but be careful where you put them. Hanging paintings above a steamy cooker is not recommended, for example. Traditionally, crockery and glassware have been displayed on Welsh dressers or in glass-fronted cabinets; for a subtler look, install rustic shelves in an unused corner of the room, so you can keep crockery and glasses close at hand without making a grand display of them. In a small space, arrange

OPPOSITE **For maximum impact, follow the example of Danish clothing desiger Naja Lauf by placing your dining table in the middle of the room and hanging a pendant light above it.**

decorative plates on a plate rack above the sink, or place vases and jugs on top of a cupboard. Artwork such as antique maps, sailor portraits or posters depicting old-fashioned beach scenes will reinforce the coastal feel in your eating area, while other features such as a mirror framed in driftwood, a leafy plant or some blue-and-white striped cushions will add freshness and vibrancy.

SLEEPING SPACES

PLAIN FURNISHINGS, SENSUOUS FABRICS AND A PALE PALETTE PREDOMINATE IN COASTAL BEDROOMS, AND DECORATIVE DETAILS ARE LIMITED TO A FEW FAVOURED ORNAMENTS AND PICTURES. BEDS, RANGING FROM ELEGANT FOUR-POSTERS TO FUTONS, OCCUPY CENTRE STAGE, WHILE MOD CONS SUCH AS TELEVISIONS ARE BANNED. INSTEAD, CRISP BEDLINEN, FLOATING DRAPES AND SIMPLE LIGHTING CREATE A SENSORY HAVEN SO THAT OUTSIDE SIGHTS AND SOUNDS — A ROSY SUNSET, WAVES CRASHING RHYTHMICALLY ONTO THE SHORE — CAN BE APPRECIATED TO THE FULL.

THIS PAGE **To create a truly restful retreat, make sure that you keep bedroom furnishings to a minimum. Calming coastal colours such as soft sand and sea green will also help to establish a meditative mood.**

FREE FORM

Ideally, coastal bedrooms should feature little more than a comfortable bed, a couple of side tables and the occasional reading lamp. Clothes and shoes should be stored out of sight. Although the look is plain and simple – bare floorboards and matt-painted walls are popular – you can create plenty of variations on the theme. Tongue-and-groove cladding is perfect for a fresh functional look, for example, while a faded kelim on polished parquet gives a cool Colonial feel.

Bedrooms are also ideal for showcasing luxurious details. If you yearn for expensive wallpaper, the boudoir is the place to indulge your desire. Choose a watered-silk style that reflects the watery setting, or nautical stripes to give a shipshape feel. If nostalgia is your thing, select a design featuring maritime motifs such as faded yachts or frilly parasols.

Limpid coastal colours come into their own in the bedroom, where the tone is muted and relaxed. Ivory, pearl, shell, oyster and other variants on white are the first choice for those wanting a soporific sanctum, while warm neutrals, including bone, biscuit, parchment, sand and mushroom, also promote tranquillity. Or combine washed-out sea and sky colours with off-whites, and introduce a minor colour accent such as pillows with a navy trim or a couple of brightly coloured ceramics.

Think carefully about the size and style of bed you want, to ensure that it's in proportion to your space as well as complementing your design scheme. For example, a modernist room with big picture windows is likely to suit simple futons, while smaller, quirkier spaces call for traditional designs such as bateaux-lits or cabin-style bunks.

A variety of different beds are suitable for coastal boudoirs, as long as they are made out of natural materials and built on simple lines, but steer clear of cumbersome four-posters, which are inimical to tranquillity, and anything too modern – chrome and leather styles are a definite no-no – since this will strike a similarly jarring note. Instead, opt for plainly elegant styles such as antique Louis XVI beds, which have caned or upholstered head- and footboards.

RIGHT **The graceful sweep of drapes falling from a four-poster bed frames a striking painting in an oval frame. Otherwise, the look is clean and uncluttered, except for a few shells arranged on the bedside table.**

FAR RIGHT **Rustic floor tiles add interest to an old-fashioned bedroom, whose few key pieces include an elegant chaise longue. Cupboards for storing clothes and shoes are relegated to the passageway, so that the sleeping space is left calm.**

OPPOSITE **The simple pencil bed and side table in a guest bedroom in the Bahamas were designed by David Flint Wood and handmade on the island.**

Modern four-posters with unadorned uprights in metal or wood also work well, as do old-fashioned iron bedsteads, which look effective in shabby-chic-style rooms. Smaller sleigh beds are perfect for children's rooms, while the clean lines and versatility of divans suit monotone minimalist spaces. Add a textural element in the form of a seersucker duvet or padded satin quilt, or customize a headboard – fretwork screens and bamboo panels work well – to create a personalized feel.

Although piles of pillows, valences and boldly patterned duvets do not suit the plain lines of coastal style, there is scope for tactile interest. For a tailored look, choose simple sheets and blankets; if possible, buy high-quality fabrics such as Egyptian cotton or Irish linen, which wears, washes and feels better than cheaper cottons that may be mixed with polyester. Linen sheets, cool to the touch, are unrivalled in intense heat. Silk sheets in plain whites or washed-out pastels are another option, while a classic quilt or vintage eiderdown suggests cosy country style.

TOP ROW, LEFT TO RIGHT **A few**
pretty accessories add a touch of style
to a coastal bedroom. A simple divan
accentuates the streamlined décor of
an airy bedroom opening onto a large
deck; the bare expanse of plain wood
floors and white-on-white bedlinen
set the tone for the minimalist look.
Necklaces designed by the Danish
jeweller Charlotte Lynggaard bring a
sparkle of feminine colour to a boudoir.

BOTTOM ROW, LEFT TO RIGHT
Pale wood flooring and a golden-yellow
colour scheme complement the sandy
shore beyond. Slim, oil-scented tapers
from India Hicks' Island Living are the
centre of an artful display. Regimented
decoration works well in minimalist
bedrooms, as long as the objects on
show echo the overall design scheme;
here, the repetition of rectangular
shapes creates its own pattern.

PREVIOUS PAGES **Floaty drapes soften the hard lines of a metal four-poster bed in an interior designed by Tom Scheerer. To create a restful feel in a bedroom, keep furnishings to a minimum, and use calming colours such as soft sand and sea green.**

OPPOSITE **Striped fabrics breathe vitality into a tonal bedroom, where beachy shades predominate. A straw hat reinforces the seaside theme.**

BELOW CENTRE **Flowers bring a sense of life and vitality to any interior.**

BELOW LEFT AND BELOW RIGHT **In a converted railway carriage, fitted bunk beds and a roughly painted wood floor recall a ship's cabin. In another room, subtly striped bedlinen and simple blinds in an equally tasteful design adorn elegant iron bedsteads.**

The boudoir offers many possibilities for showcasing fabrics. Tasselled throws, loose covers, ethereal drapes and the occasional cushion all help to give design schemes a sense of direction. Enhance the look with simple white or striped blinds, or add a textural element with grass or bamboo styles. By the same token, white or off-white lampshades in paper or opaque parchment will subtly complement silk or cotton sheets. Muslin bed drapes work particularly well in coastal bedrooms, giving an exotic feel that softens harsh minimalist lines. To get the look, simply attach lengths of semi-transparent fabric from the corners of a four-poster bed, or hang a drop of sheer fabric from a large hook or corona in the ceiling.

BATHING SPACES

BATHROOMS ARE UTILITARIAN SPACES, BUT THEY CAN ALSO BE COMFORTABLE AND STYLISH. INDEED, MODERN BATHROOMS ARE FAST BECOMING THE ULTIMATE PLEASURE ZONE — A SANCTUARY FOR BODY AND SOUL. WHETHER YOU HAVE A SIMPLE SHOWER ROOM OR A BATHROOM LARGE ENOUGH TO ACCOMMODATE A FREESTANDING TUB AND A COUPLE OF ARMCHAIRS TO BOOT, TRY TO MAKE THE MOST OF SEA VIEWS AND HARNESS AS MUCH NATURAL LIGHT AS POSSIBLE, WHILE CREATING A SPACE THAT IS FUNCTIONAL AND FRESH. THE SIMPLER AND MORE UNCLUTTERED YOU CAN MAKE YOUR BATHING SPACE, THE EASIER IT WILL BE FOR YOU TO FEEL RELAXED AND REVITALIZED.

WASHED IN LIGHT

As any seaside-dweller will tell you, the wraparound views of sea and sky are among the chief delights of coastal living – and a bathroom is a wonderful place from which to appreciate a shimmering ocean vista. After all, what could be nicer than watching the waves as you wallow in the tub?

If you are designing a bathroom from scratch and are lucky enough to have a big window, put your bath directly beneath it, so that you can enjoy the views while allowing daylight to flow into the space around you. Alternatively, place the bath at right angles to the window or, if you have a large bathroom, in the centre of the room facing directly onto it.

Even if your room lacks a large window, you can make a link with the outdoors. In a top-floor room, for example, install a skylight, so that you can watch the clouds passing as you bathe. For a nautical touch, replace small windows with portholes; for a tropical-island feel, install shutters or louvred blinds; or, if your bathroom is overlooked, add muslin drapes to act as pretty, light-filtering screens.

Light-reflective fixtures and fittings are another way to create an airy bathing space. For an ultra-modern feel, replace existing doors with reinforced-glass ones to usher in light from the landing (or bedroom if your bathroom is en suite). Doors fitted with semi-opaque panels are another option for those who want to maintain privacy. If you have a large bathroom, glass partitions can be used to divide up space without impeding the flow of light.

There are many types of glass finishes available, including sandblasted, etched, printed and textured. Opaque-glass bricks are a fashionable way to screen off private areas such as a shower or loo, while tinted glass in gentle blues and greens gives an aquatic feel. Natural daylight can be maximized by angling mirrors so that they bounce light around the room; similarly, installing light-reflective chrome and glass fittings will enhance the fresh, functional feel.

Coastal-style bathrooms need resilient, non-slip, hardwearing floors. Natural flooring such as stone, cork and timber is marvellous for enhancing the

TOP LEFT **A combination of off-white wall tiles, a plain linoleum floor and a vintage-style shower creates an old-fashioned, utilitarian feel.**

TOP CENTRE **Quirky decorative accessories such as this carved stone heart prevent bathrooms from appearing too functional.**

TOP RIGHT **Siting a bath under a big window is a great way to bring the outside in; the sea-green walls and floor enhance the natural feel.**

ABOVE LEFT **Tongue-and-groove panelling painted pale grey instils a sense of freshness and harmonizes with the grey-painted bathtub.**

ABOVE CENTRE **Offbeat items such as a shuttered mirror and a decorative wrought-iron chair jazz up a plain white bathing space.**

ABOVE RIGHT **Greenery energizes bathing spaces, as well as helping to maintain a link between inside and out.**

ROUGH-HEWN WALLS ECHO THE
RUGGEDNESS OF ANCIENT CLIFFS,
WHILE SLEEK FINISHES SUCH AS
MARBLE, LIMESTONE AND PLASTER
RECALL SURF-POLISHED PEBBLES.

PREVIOUS PAGES AND RIGHT
A bath beside a large window is the ultimate luxury, especially in a remote location where curtains or blinds are not required to protect privacy. In this home designed by Stelle Architects, a ceramic bath and shiny taps enhance the airy feel. If your room looks out over the sea, make sure that the fixtures and fittings are as streamlined as possible, so as not to detract from the view. To reinforce the look, use colours that reflect the watery scenery.

FAR RIGHT Modern design schemes tend to work best when flooded with natural sunlight. Green foliage outside the window is another plus, helping to soften the hard lines of boxy ceramic basins and built-in storage.

OPPOSITE Wet rooms are a popular alternative to traditional bathing spaces. Here, non-slip slate floor tiles and sleek shower fittings have been combined with a masculine brown-and-white colour scheme in the Danish home of Charlotte Lynggaard.

outside-in look – but avoid parquet, bamboo and wood-laminate floors since these tend to warp when wet. Instead, choose tough vinyl tiles, which can be arranged in a chequerboard pattern to give a shipshape feel. Wall treatments are equally versatile, ranging from roughly finished stone to cool marble. Not surprisingly, relatively inexpensive tongue-and-groove wooden panelling is a perennial favourite, recalling the streamlined chic of beach huts.

A watery palette works well in coastal bathrooms. Use specially formulated bathroom paint in limpid shades of blue, green, grey and off-white. These calming colours complement a wide variety of furniture, from wood to stainless steel, and help to create a sense of serenity.

Antique-style sanitaryware is a good option for rustic bathrooms. Reclamation yards are an excellent place to source restored basins and baths, and attractive reproduction sanitaryware is also widely available. Good-quality new taps and shower heads will pull the look together.

THIS PAGE Rustic furnishings tend
to suit smaller bathing spaces, where
a cosy, self-contained feel is required.
Here, a simple Shaker peg rail neatly
complements an antique model yacht
and a flimsy curtain patterned with
old-fashioned cabbage-rose motifs.

OPPOSITE Stripped wooden boards
and tongue-and-groove panelling give
an impression of space in this unique
bathroom, which was converted from
an old railway carriage. The opaque
glass door and etched smoking sign
are further reminders of days gone by.

SERVICE

OPPOSITE Sunny-coloured marble gives this room by Tom Scheerer a warm glow. Furnishings are minimal, so that most of the visual interest derives from the textural grain of the plain wood cabinet and the grey striations in the stone.

RIGHT There is a multitude of ways to create a beachy feel in coastal bathrooms – from displaying the odd decorative shell to hanging a mirror framed in driftwood. Here, the look is achieved through the addition of a simple basket and a shell necklace.

Freestanding cast-iron baths exude a vintage feel, thanks to their elegant claw feet and softly curving edges, which are reminiscent of faded grandeur. To enhance the look, choose unconventional basins – a ceramic bowl set on a wooden table, for example.

Seaside bathrooms offer the ideal showcase for decorative marine details. Scallop-shaped soap dishes, mirrors framed in driftwood and glass jars filled with shells usher in a sense of the seashore, while bathing accessories such as loofahs, sponges and pumice stones extend the theme. Although all have a functional role, towels, shower curtains and bath mats can also bring colour and interest into a bathroom. A boldly striped bath sheet adds a bright, beachy note, for example, as does a shower curtain patterned with starfish or sailing boats. Introducing textural details is another way to liven up neutrally decorated bathrooms. Sisal storage baskets will soften the harsh edges of glass and chrome fixtures and fittings, while a bamboo towel rail or waffle-weave bath mat add a subtle layer of interest. Finally, don't forget to include flowers and plants – a vase of casually arranged blooms or a spiky cactus will literally breathe life into your bathroom.

OUTDOOR SPACES

A FABULOUS OUTDOOR SPACE IS ONE OF THE MOST IMPORTANT INGREDIENTS OF SUCCESSFUL SEASIDE LIVING. AFTER ALL, WHAT IS THE POINT OF LIVING BY THE OCEAN IF YOU ARE NOT GOING TO SPEND TIME COMMUNING WITH NATURE? IT GOES WITHOUT SAYING THAT YOUR EXTERNAL SPACE SHOULD BE AS WELL DESIGNED AS YOUR INTERIOR ONE, BUT THIS DOESN'T MEAN THAT IT NEEDS TO BE OSTENTATIOUS. WHEN IT COMES TO APPRECIATING THE BEAUTY OF THE SEA AND SKY, A SIMPLE SALT-STAINED DECK OR A SMALL FLOWER-FILLED PATIO WILL DO THE JOB JUST AS EFFECTIVELY AS A SPRAWLING VERANDA OR A GARDEN BURSTING WITH BOUGAINVILLEA.

ABOVE AND OPPOSITE **Thick tropical foliage makes a lush backdrop to two outdoor rooms designed by Tom Scheerer. Arching rafters, delicate trellising and a central ceiling fan all create a breezy feel on the terrace shown above. The mainly woody look of the open-ended sitting area opposite is enlivened by bright cushions and a pair of graphic side tables.**

To enjoy the vista from your coastal home in comfort and style, you need a viewing platform in the shape of a deck, balcony, terrace or veranda. Timber decking is an ideal complement to large expanses of wood, metal and glass. A shady veranda is another option, offering an elegant setting for a couple of rocking chairs and the occasional drinks trolley, while patios and terraces adjoining the house are excellent for outside entertaining. If you are building a terrace from scratch, stick to indigenous materials that replicate the fabric of your home. This will provide a sense of seamless continuity and help to make your outdoor

space appear like another room. Paving stones and brickwork are ideal, while funkier alternatives such as a small, pebbled-filled area are effective for establishing a visual connection with the beach.

Furniture should match the setting. A weathered Adirondack-style chair complements salt-stained decking, for example, while swing seats look good in rambling gardens. Outdoor furnishings can make or break a look, so choose wood or metal items rather than flimsy loungers or lightweight plastic tables. Although naturally hard-wearing materials are costlier than manmade ones, they suit the integrity of coastal style.

OVERLEAF **David Flint Wood and India Hicks have adorned the veranda of their guest house in the Bahamas with fresh white paintwork and classic wicker furniture. Outdoor living in the Caribbean depends on overhanging roofs that offer protection from tropical downpours as well as from the sun.**

ABOVE, LEFT TO RIGHT White timber cladding and a matching table and chairs give an orderly feel to a balcony. Striped cushions and plain tableware set the scene for alfresco dining. A sturdy table and elegant metal chairs are a good choice for a modernist deck; a vast pot of flowers adds a summery feel. Folding metal chairs are a perennial favourite in outside spaces; mix and match them to add interest to a plain wooden table.

RIGHT AND FAR RIGHT Wooden furnishings and a white parasol make the perfect complement to a minimalist deck designed by Stelle Architects. A tablecloth billows in the wind, while pebbles anchor the napkins and prevent them from being blown away.

BELOW LEFT **If you want the flaky-paint look but can't wait for nature to take its course, buy vintage pieces instead of new ones. This old recliner in the corner of a deck has been given a new lease of life through the addition of a reconditioned canvas seat.**

BELOW CENTRE **Although they look fragile, daisies thrive in salty habitats. Mix them with lavender, a similarly hardy plant, to soften the hard lines of decks and balconies. Delicate florals also provide a lush contrast to the dry scrubland of coastal environments.**

BELOW RIGHT **A linear table with benches on either side is a practical option for hospitable coast-dwellers or those with large families. Table settings are kept simple – with white ceramic plates and clear glass tumblers the most popular choice.**

OPPOSITE **Rustic details set the scene in outside dining areas. Here, a pretty brick wall makes the perfect backdrop for an old-fashioned gas lamp and a weatherbeaten table. A bowl of onions and a dented metal vase complete the pastoral picture.**

If you want an immediately authentic look, scour antiques markets and second-hand shops for attractively distressed tables, chairs and recliners, which will effortlessly blend in with the environment.

Parasols, awnings and canopies in weather-resistant acrylic cloth are vital, providing relief from the glare of the sun. Good choices include light sunny shades and brightly striped fabrics that can be mixed and matched with deckchairs or hammocks in similarly jaunty designs.

BELOW **An overgrown garden suits the relaxed informality of coastal style and provides a harmonious setting for elegant outdoor furnishings such as a simple slatted bench.**

BELOW RIGHT **Outside spaces don't have to be sleek to be successful. Here, an old metal table framed by lavender bushes is used to display coastal treasures including a group of shells and a length of rope.**

Soft furnishings help to offset hard surfaces in outdoor living areas and promote a sense of comfort. Fabrics for upholstery and seat pads should be tough enough to withstand damp, salty environments – cotton canvas, ticking and towelling are all ideal. Strong colours and bold shapes look at home by the sea, so if you have a yen for loud stripes or splashy jungle prints, indulge it here. Otherwise, stick to a tonal palette of blues, greens, browns and greys, to harmonize with the landscape.

Eating alfresco is one of the most enjoyable aspects of outdoor living. Regardless of whether you are throwing a large, candlelit dinner party or hosting a leisurely family lunch, the mood should always be one

of relaxed informality. If you are sitting down for a meal around a table, make sure that it is high enough for guests' knees to fit comfortably underneath. Another option is to replace chairs with refectory-style benches topped with seat pads or a single flat box cushion filled with thick foam. This allows you to accommodate more people around the table and is excellent for large social gatherings.

To achieve an eclectic look, mix and match different chair designs – contemporary pieces in rustic styles and one-off commissions work well. Otherwise, choose fold-up metal chairs with painted wooden slats; these are popular among coastal homeowners because they are

BELOW **An old bench is shown off to good effect against a backdrop of trailing greenery. Wooden or metal benches become more beautiful over time as a result of the weathering effects of sun and wind.**

BELOW LEFT **The curves of a sunbleached lounger complement the elegant lines of a swimming pool. David Flint Wood's planting creates a vista along an avenue of coconut trees.**

OPPOSITE Sand and salt are an integral part of coastal life, which is why a shower is a big advantage in outdoor living spaces. At this home in the Bahamas, a makeshift cubicle, built out of densely packed bamboo, makes a great private sluicing area.

THIS PAGE If you are building a beach house from scratch, you may want to follow the example of Stelle Architects, who designed this house on Long Island, and include high-tech washing facilities such as a power shower, sauna, hot tub or steam room.

portable, attractive and hardwearing: To complete the scene, simply attach pretty seat pads to the backs of chairs and drape a matching cloth over a garden table. Tableware should be eclectic. Combine white china with clear glass for a sophisticated look, or, for a more casual effect, mix bright plastic and acrylic picnicware with hand-painted ceramics, raffia mats and a jar of assorted cutlery.

Entertaining by night should be similarly relaxed. To maintain a sense of continuity with your interior, use a variety of lighting so that your outside space looks like a cosy room. The mood that prevails in your outdoor area depends on the type of lighting you choose. Floodlights on paths and steps will give a practical but stylish feel, for example, while spotlights among the plants light up foliage and create interesting shadows. To create a party mood, twine a simple string of fairylights through the railings of your deck or balcony, or hang some colourful candle jar lights from a garden umbrella. Alternatively, use votive candles to provide a pretty flickering glow or decorate your table with slim tapers arranged in clusters.

THIS PAGE **Alfresco bathing is
one of the many delights of seaside
living, enabling coastal-dwellers to
feel at one with the sea and sky. In
this outdoor space, a boxed-in bath
merges seamlessly with the linear
decking, while its basic design is
appropriate to the salty setting.**

THE ENDLESS POTENTIAL TO BLUR THE BOUNDARIES BETWEEN INDOORS AND OUT IS ONE OF THE MOST APPEALING ASPECTS OF LIVING BESIDE THE SEA.

SOURCES

Anthropologie
www.anthropologie.com
One-of-a-kind home accessories, from decorative hooks and boxes to pillows and throws.

Baileys Home & Garden
www.baileyshomeand
garden.com
Inspired homewares by mail order, including recycled glass floats, coir fenders, driftwood, pebbles and outdoor lights.

Beach Dwelling
www.beachdwelling.com
(+1) 800 941 9690
Online store selling homewares inspired by coastal living.

The Beach Hut
www.beachhut.co.uk
(+44) 01892 557964
Stylish coastal accessories by mail order.

Benjamin Moore Paints
www.benjaminmoore.com
Fine paints.Visit the website for details of stockists

Buy the Sea
www.buythesea.co.uk
(+44) 01460 258970
Gifts and home accessories with a nautical theme by mail order.

Côté Jardin
Place du Marché
17590 Ares en Ré
France
(+33) 05 46 29 29 61
Decoration and brocante for house and garden.

Crate and Barrel
www.crateandbarrel.com
(+1) 800 967 6696
A wide choice of housewares and furniture suited to coastal homes. Visit the website to find a store near you.

Crucial Trading
www.crucial-trading.com
(+44) 01562 743747
Wide range of natural floor coverings in sisal, seagrass and jute.

Farrow & Ball
www.farrow-ball.com
Historic paint colours and wallpapers. Visit the website for details of stockists worldwide.

Fired Earth
www.firedearth.com
(+44) 0845 366 0400
Tiled and wooden flooring.

Ian Mankin
271/273 Wandsworth
Bridge Road
London SW6 2TX
www.ianmankin.com
(+44) 020 7722 0997
Striped fabrics and ticking.

Jan Constantine
www.janconstantine.com
(+44) 01270 821194
Hand-embroidered fabrics and beautiful accessories for seaside homes.

Laura Ashley
www.lauraashley.com
(+44) 0871 983 5999
Home furnishings, paint and fabrics with colourways and ranges that recall the seaside. Visit the website to find a store near you.

The Lexington Company
www.lexingtoncompany.com
Items for bedroom and bathroom including an exclusive American Seaside range.

The Linen Works
www.thelinenworks.com
(+44) 020 7819 7620
Striped fabrics and a range of homewares for kitchen, dining, living and bedroom by mail order.

Seaside Treasures and More, Inc.
www.seasidetreasures.com
(+1) 727 943 3970
Wide range of nautical home accessories including, lanterns, clocks, flags and lobster traps.

Newport Nautical Decor
www.newportnauticaldecor.com
Furniture and accessories designed for cottage homes beside the sea.

Ocean Interiors
www.oceaninteriors.ca
Furniture and decorative items for coastal homes and seaside living.

Pebble
www.pebblelondon.com
191 Sussex Gardens
London W2 2RH
(+44) 020 7262 1775
Exquisite range of shells, shell jewellery and other decorative pieces.

Pottery Barn
www.potterybarn.com
(+1) 888 779 5176
Contemporary furniture and accessories for the home. Visit the website to find a store near you.

Ralph Lauren Home
www.rlhome.polo.com
(+1) 888 475 7674
Furniture and fabrics that combine rusticity with elegance. Visit the website to find a store near you.

Re
www.re-foundobjects.com
(+44) 01434 634567
New and antique decorative accessories including many unusual pieces perfect for coastal living.

Restoration Hardware
www.restorationhardware.com
935 Broadway
New York, NY 10010
(+1) 212 260 9479
Fine hardware, including lighting; also furniture and home accessories. Visit the website to find a store near you.

Shutters Beach Style
www.shuttersbeachstyle.com
(+1) 888 334 9110
Accessories and gifts on a maritime theme.

The Shell Shop
www.theshellshop.net
590 Embarcadero
Morro Bay, CA 93442
USA
(+1) 805 772 8014
A wide selection of shells and decorative shell accessories.

Southsea Deckchairs
www.deckchairs.co.uk
(+44) 02392 652865
Wide range of different styles of deckchair.

Trinidad
www.trinidad.fr
Route de la Prée
17590 Ars en Ré
France
(+33) 0546 29 41 36
Beautifully designed and crafted teak sun loungers and deck chairs for outdoor living.

The White Company
www.thewhitecompany.com
(+44) 0844 736 4222
High-quality bedlinen and stylish home accessories. Visit the website to order online or locate your nearest store.

West Elm
www.westelm.com
(+1) 888 922 4119
Online Williams-Sonoma store offering many homewares suitable for coastal living.

PICTURE CREDITS

All photography by Paul Massey.
key: a=above, b=below, l=left, r=right, c=centre.

Page 1 Jan Constantine – www.janconstantine.com; 6 a house in the Bahamas designed by Tom Scheerer; 13, 14 al, bl & br Stelle Architects: Surfside, a small family compound nestled in the dunes at the water's edge; 14 ac, cl, cr & bc David Flint Wood & India Hicks' home in The Bahamas; 14 ar Jan Constantine – www.janconstantine.com; 14 c Stelle Architects: Dune House, a renovated and expanded 'spec' house behind the dunes near the ocean; 16 l & r Stelle Architects: a 19th-century summerhouse brought into the 21st century; 16 c Michael Giannelli & Greg Shano's home in East Hampton; 17 (all) the home in Denmark of Charlotte Lynggaard, designer, of Ole Lynggaard Copenhagen; 18 l Jane Packer's home in Suffolk; 18 c & ar Tom Scheerer; 18 br & 19 the Bartons' seaside home in West Sussex: www.thedodo.co.uk; 21 all items from Côté Jardin boutique; 22 al, ar & c, Hôtel Le Sénéchal, Ars en Ré, designed by Christophe Ducharme Architecte – items on mantelpiece and side table (22c) from Côté Jardin boutique; 22 ac & bc Hotel Tresanton, St Mawes, Cornwall owned and designed by Olga Polizzi; 22 cl all items from Côté Jardin boutique; 22 cr Stelle Architects: a 19th-century summerhouse brought into the 21st century; 22 bl & br private residence, Denmark; 24–25 designed by Olga Polizzi; 26 a house in Ile de Ré; 27 Hôtel Le Sénéchal, Ars en Ré, designed by Christophe Ducharme Architecte; 29, 30 ac & c, David Flint Wood & India Hicks' home in The Bahamas; 30 al, bl & br all items from Côté Jardin boutique; 30 ar Hotel Tresanton, St Mawes, Cornwall, owned and designed by Olga Polizzi; 30 cl & cr Jane Packer's home in Suffolk; 30 bc & 32 Hôtel Le Sénéchal, Ars en Ré, designed by Christophe Ducharme Architecte; 33 l David Flint Wood & India Hicks' home in The Bahamas; 33 c Cote Jardin boutique; 33 r Stelle Architects: Dune House, a renovated and expanded 'spec' house behind the dunes near the ocean; 34 Tom Scheerer; 35 Hotel Tresanton, St Mawes, Cornwall, owned and designed by Olga Polizzi; 38 al the Bartons' seaside home in West Sussex: www.thedodo.co.uk; 38 ac & cl Jan Constantine – www.janconstantine.com; 38 ar Jane Packer's home in Suffolk; 38 cr & 38 bl The Spreitzer residence, Southampton, New York; 38 br the home in Denmark of Charlotte Lynggaard, designer, of Ole Lynggaard Copenhagen; 43 Michael Giannelli & Greg Shano's home in East Hampton; 44, 45 c & r David Flint Wood & India Hicks' home in The Bahamas; 45 l & 49 all items from Côté Jardin Jardin boutique; 52–53a Jane Packer's home in Suffolk; 53 bl Jan Constantine – www.janconstantine.com; 53 ar & 54 Côté Jardin boutique; 55 l the home in Denmark of Charlotte Lynggaard, designer, of Ole Lynggaard Copenhagen; 55r Jane Packer's home in Suffolk; 56 Jan Constantine – www. janconstantine.com; 57 Côté Jardin boutique; 58 l, 61, 62 a & c (all) the home in Denmark of Charlotte Lynggaard, designer, of Ole Lynggaard; 62bl Hotel Tresanton, St Mawes, Cornwall owned and designed by Olga Polizzi; 62 bc Jan Constantine-www.janconstantine.com; 62 br Côté Jardin boutique; 64–65 (all) Jan Constantine – www.janconstantine.com; 66 the home in Denmark of Charlotte Lynggaard, designer, of Ole Lynggaard; 67 l & c Jan Constantine – www.janconstantine.com; 67r Naja Lauf; 69 & 70 c Michael Giannelli & Greg Shano's home in East Hampton; 70 al Olga Polizzi; 70 ac & cr Jane Packer's home in Suffolk; 70 ar & bl all items from Côté Jardin boutique; 70 cl &

br David Flint Wood & India Hicks' home in The Bahamas; 70 bc & 72 Jan Constantine – www.janconstantine.com; 73 l Hôtel Le Sénéchal, Ars en Ré, designed by Christophe Ducharme Architecte; 73 c, 73 r, 74 l & 74 c all items from Côté Jardin boutique; 74 r private residence, Denmark; 75 & 76–77 a David Flint Wood & India Hicks' home in The Bahamas; 76 b & 77 r all items from Côté Jardin boutique; 77 bl a house in the Bahamas designed by Tom Scheerer; 78 Naja Lauf; 79 private residence, Denmark; 80 Michael Giannelli & Greg Shano's home in East Hampton; 81 l the Bartons' seaside home in West Sussex: www.thedodo.co.uk; 81 r Hôtel Le Sénéchal, Ars en Ré, designed by Christophe Ducharme Architecte; 82 al all items from Côté Jardin boutique; 82 ac & 83 bc the home in Denmark of Charlotte Lynggaard, designer, of Ole Lynggaard; 82 ar, bc & br a house in the Bahamas designed by Tom Scheerer; 82br The Spreitzer residence, Southampton, New York; 83 al David Flint Wood & India Hicks' home in The Bahamas; 83 ac Hôtel Le Sénéchal, Ars en Ré, designed by Christophe Ducharme Architecte; 83 ar the Barton's seaside home in West Sussex: www.thedodo.co.uk; 83 bl Jan Constantine – www.janconstantine.com; 83 br Tom Scheerer; 85 private residence, Denmark; 86 & 87 c all items from Côté Jardin boutique; 87 l Stelle Architects: Surfside, a small family compound nestled in the dunes at the water's edge; 87 r a house in Ile de Ré; 88 the Bartons' seaside home in West Sussex: www.thedodo.co.uk; 89 the home in Denmark of Charlotte Lynggaard, designer, of Ole Lynggaard; 90–91 & 91 br private residence, Denmark; 91 ar & cr Naja Lauf; 92 (both) Hotel Tresanton, St Mawes, Cornwall, owned and designed by Olga Polizzi; 93 David Flint Wood & India Hicks' home in The Bahamas; 94–95 a house in the Bahamas designed by Tom Scheerer; 96 & 97 (all) David Flint Wood & India Hicks' home in The Bahamas; 99 Naja Lauf; 100 Tom Scheerer; 101, all images, all items from Côté Jardin boutique; 102–103 The Spreitzer residence, Southampton, New York; 104 al & br Michael Giannelli & Greg Shano's home in East Hampton; 104 ac Stelle Architects: Surfside, a small family compound nestled in the dunes at the water's edge; 104 ar a house in the Bahamas designed by Tom Scheerer; 104 bl David Flint Wood & India Hicks' home in The Bahamas; 104 bc & 105 private residence, Denmark; 106 & 107 l the home in Denmark of Charlotte Lynggaard, designer, of Ole Lynggaard; 107r Michael Giannelli & Greg Shano's home in East Hampton; 108–109 Jane Packer's home in Suffolk; 110–11 a house in the Bahamas designed by Tom Scheerer; 112 Naja Lauf; 113 l The Spreitzer residence, Southampton, New York; 113 c & r the Bartons' seaside home in West Sussex: www.thedodo.co.uk; 115 Michael Giannelli & Greg Shano's home in East Hampton; 116 A house in Ile de Ré; 118 & 119 David Flint Wood & India Hicks' home in The Bahamas; 120 al & ac Stelle Architects: Surfside, a small family compound nestled in the dunes at the water's edge; 120 b Stelle Architects: Dune House, a renovated and expanded 'spec' house behind the dunes near the ocean; 120–21 a the home in Denmark of Charlotte Lynggaard, designer, of Ole Lynggaard; 121 bl & br David Flint Wood & India Hicks' home in The Bahamas; 122–23 Tom Scheerer; 124 &125 the Bartons' seaside home in West Sussex: www.thedodo.co.uk; 127 Michael Giannelli & Greg Shano's home in East Hampton;

129 al, ac & br Naja Lauf; 129 ar private residence, Denmark; 129 bl Jan Constantine – www.janconstantine.com; 129 bc David Flint Wood & India Hicks' home in The Bahamas; 130–31 Stelle Architects: Dune House, a renovated and expanded 'spec' house behind the dunes near the ocean; 132 & 133 r the home in Denmark of Charlotte Lynggaard, designer, of Ole Lynggaard; 133 l Stelle Architects: Dune House, a renovated and expanded 'spec' house behind the dunes near the ocean; 134 & 135 the Bartons' seaside home in West Sussex: www.thedodo.co.uk; 136 a house in the Bahamas designed by Tom Scheerer; 137 Tom Scheerer; 139 Stelle Architects: Surfside, a small family compound nestled in the dunes at the water's edge; 140 a house in the Bahamas designed by Tom Scheerer; 141 Tom Scheerer; 142–43 David Flint Wood & India Hicks' home in The Bahamas; 144 l Naja Lauf; 144 ar the home in Denmark of Charlotte Lynggaard, designer, of Ole Lynggaard; 144–45 b

Stelle Architects: Dune House, a renovated and expanded 'spec' house behind the dunes near the ocean; 145 al Hotel Tresanton, St Mawes, Cornwall owned and designed by Olga Polizzi; 145 ar the Bartons' seaside home in West Sussex: www.thedodo.co.uk; 145 br Jan Constantine – www.janconstantine.com; 146 l & 146 r Hôtel Le Sénéchal, Ars en Ré, designed by Christophe Ducharme Architecte; 146 c & 147 Naja Lauf; 148 l Jane Packer's home in Suffolk; 148 r Côté Jardin boutique; 149 l David Flint Wood & India Hicks' home in The Bahamas; 149 r Stelle Architects: a 19th-century summerhouse brought into the 21st century; 150 Tom Scheerer; 151 Stelle Architects: Surfside, a small family compound nestled in the dunes at the water's edge; 152–53 the Bartons' seaside home in West Sussex: www.thedodo.co.uk; 157 & 160 r David Flint Wood & India Hicks' home in The Bahamas; 160 l the Bartons' seaside home in West Sussex: www.thedodo.co.uk.

BUSINESS CREDITS for locations featured in this book

key: a=above, b=below, l=left, r=right, c=centre.

Côté Jardin (boutique)
Place du Marche
17590 Ars En Re
France
+ 33 (0)5 46 29 29 61
Pages 21, 22 cl, 30 al, 30 bl, 30 br, 33 c, 38 c, 38 bc, 45 l, 49, 53 ar, 54, 57, 62 br, 70 ar, 70 bl, 73 c, 73 r, 74 l, 74 c, 76 b, 77 r, 82 al, 86, 87 c, 101 all, 148 r.

The Dodo
www.thedodo.co.uk
Pages 18 br, 19, 38 al, 81 l, 83 ar, 88, 113 c, 113 r, 124, 125, 134, 135, 145 ar, 152–53, 160 l.

Hôtel Le Sénéchal
6, rue Gambetta
17590 Ars en Ré
France
+ 33 (0)5 46 29 40 42
www.hotel-le-senechal.com
designed by:
Christophe Ducharme
Architecte
15 rue Hégésippe Moreau
75018 Paris
France
+ 33 (0)1 45 22 07 75
Pages 22 al, 22 ar, 22 c, 27, 30 bc, 32, 73 l, 81 r, 83 ac, 146 l, 146 r.

Hotel Tresanton
St Mawes
Cornwall
01326 270055
www.tresanton.com
Olga Polizzi – owner and interior designer
Pages 22 ac, 22 bc, 24, 25, 30 ar, 35, 62 bl, 70 al, 92 both, 145 al.

India Hicks' Island Living
www.indiahicks-islandliving.com
for India Hicks' Island Living Products.
The Pavilion and The Guest House at Hibiscus Hill are occasionally available for rent:
www.hibiscushill harbourisland.com
Pages 14 ac, 14 cl, 14 cr, 14 bc, 29, 30 ac, 30 c, 33 l, 44, 45 c, 45 r, 70 cl, 70 br, 75, 76–77 a, 83 al, 93, 96, 97, 104 bl, 118, 119, 121 bl, 121 br, 129 bc, 142–43, 149 l, 157, 160 r.

Jan Constantine
01270 821194
www.janconstantine.com
Pages 1, 14 ar, 38 ac, 38 cl, 53 bl, 56, 62 bc, 64, 65, 67 l, 67 c, 70 bc, 72, 83 bl, 129 bl, 145 br.

Jane Packer
London–Tokyo–New York
www.jane-packer.co.uk
Pages 18 l, 30 cl, 30 cr, 38 ar, 52–53 a, 55 r, 70 ac, 70 cr, 108, 109, 148 l.

Naja Lauf A/S
Strandvejen 340
DK–2930 Klampenborg
+ 45 7025 1325
www.najalauf.com
Pages 67 r, 78, 91 ar, 91 cr, 99, 112, 129 al, 129 ac, 129 br, 144 l, 146 c, 147.

Ole Lynggaard Copenhagen
Flagship store:
NY Østergade 4
1101 København K
+ 45 33 33 03 45
www.olelynggaard.com
Pages 17 all, 38 br, 55 l, 58 l, 61, 62 a, 62 c, 66, 82 ac, 83 bc, 89, 106, 107 l, 120–21a, 132, 133 r, 144 ar.

Philip de Givenchy
(doors & windows)
Atmosphere
pdgatmosphere@hotmail.com
Pages 6, 77 bl, 82 ar, 82 bc, 82 br, 94–95, 104 ar, 110, 111, 136, 140.

Private residence, Denmark
Kitchen by Rasmus Larsson
Design By Us
www.design-by-us.com
also summer house in South of France to rent:
www.villalagachon.com
Pages 22 bl, 22 br, 59 l, 74 r, 79, 85, 90–91, 91 br, 104 bc, 105, 129 ar.

Stelle Architects
48 Foster Avenue
PO Box 3002
Bridgehampton, NY 11932
USA
+ 1 631 537 0019
www.stelleco.com
Pages 13, 14 al, 14 bl, 14 br, 14 c, 16 l, 16 r, 22 cr, 33 r, 87 l, 104 ac, 120 al, 120 ac, 120 b, 130–31, 133 l, 139, 144–45 b, 149 r, 151.

Tom Scheerer Inc.
New York
info@tomscheerer.com
Pages 6, 18 c, 18 ar, 34, 77 bl, 82 ar, 82 bc, 82 br, 83 br, 94–95, 100, 104 ar, 110, 111, 122–23, 136, 137, 140, 141, 150.

INDEX

Figures in *italics* denote captions/illustrations only.

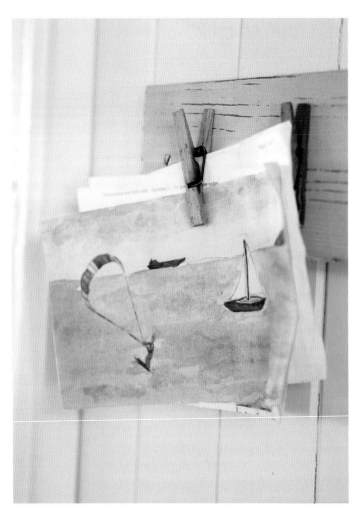

AUTHOR'S ACKNOWLEDGMENTS

Thank you to everyone who has worked tirelessly on this book – through rain, hail and shine. I should like to thank in particular the team at Ryland Peters & Small who made the book possible – Alison Starling for commissioning it in the first place and for her continued support and enthusiasm; Pamela Daniels and Henrietta Heald for designing and editing the book and making it look amazing; and Emily Westlake for her hard work and dedication in securing our locations.

Special thanks are due to all the owners, architects and designers who let us photograph their fabulous coastal homes, especially the team at Stelle Architects in the Hamptons for their time and effort in showing us their projects; to Michael Giannelli, who organized the interstate shipment of beautiful roses for our shoot; to David Flint Wood, India Hicks and Tom Scheerer in the Bahamas for being so helpful and hospitable; and to everyone on the Ile de Ré – Marina Ducharme at Hôtel Le Sénéchal, Valérie Dawlat-Dumoulin at Trinidad, and the Madec family for access to their home and all their wonderful props from Côté Jardin. Thank you also to Jane Packer and Jan Constantine for taking the time to be with us on our shoots, and to Frederica Bertolini and her team at Hotel Tresanton.

Sally Hayden